C000150671

ECDL ®

European Computer Driving Licence®

Word Processing Software
BCS ITQ Level 1

Using Microsoft® Word 2010

Syllabus Version 2.0

This training, which has been approved by BCS, includes exercise items intended to assist learners in their training for a BCS or ECDL Certification Programme. These exercises are not certification tests. For information about how to take a certification test and to find Approved Centres in the UK, please refer to the BCS website at www.bcs.org/qualifications.

Release ITQ150v1

Published by:

CiA Training Ltd
Business & Innovation Centre
Sunderland Enterprise Park
Sunderland
SR5 2TA
United Kingdom

Tel: +44 (0) 191 549 5002
Fax: +44 (0) 191 549 9005

E-mail: info@ciatraining.co.uk
Web: www.ciatraining.co.uk

ISBN: 978-0-85741-046-7

Important Notes

This guide was written for *Microsoft Office 2010* running on *Windows 7*. If using a different version of *Windows* some dialog boxes may look and function slightly differently to that described. It is also assumed file extensions are enabled in *Windows*, which is important for demonstrating the differences between file types.

To turn on file extensions, click the **Start** button and open the **Control Panel**. From **Appearance and Personalization** select **Folder Options**, and then from the dialog box click the **View** tab and uncheck **Hide extensions for known file types**. Click **OK**.

A resolution of *1024x768* was also used to produce screenshots for this guide. Working at a different resolution (or with an application window which is not maximised) may change the look of the dynamic *Office Ribbon*, which changes to fit the space available.

For example, the **Editing Group** on a full *Ribbon* will contain several buttons, but if space is restricted it may be replaced by an **Editing Button** (which, when clicked, will display the full **Editing Group**).

First published 2013

Copyright © 2013 CiA Training Ltd

All rights reserved. No part of this publication may be reproduced, stored in a retrieval system, or transmitted in any form or by any means (electronic, mechanical, photocopying, recording or otherwise) without the prior written permission of CiA Training Limited.

Microsoft is a registered trademark and Windows is a trademark of the Microsoft Corporation. Screen images reproduced by permission of the Microsoft Corporation. All other trademarks in this book are acknowledged as the property of their respective owners.

European Computer Driving Licence, ECDL, International Computer Driving Licence, ICDL, and related logos are all registered Trade Marks of The European Computer Driving Licence Foundation Limited ("ECDL Foundation").

CiA Training Ltd is an entity independent of The British Computer Society using the name BCS, The Chartered Institute for IT ("BCS") and is not associated with ECDL Foundation or BCS in any manner.

This courseware may be used to assist learners to prepare for the ECDL Certification Programme as titled on the courseware. Neither BCS nor **CiA Training Ltd** warrants that the use of this courseware publication will ensure passing of the tests for that ECDL Certification Programme.

This courseware publication has been independently reviewed and approved by BCS as covering the learning objectives for the ECDL Certification Programme.

Confirmation of this approval can be obtained by reviewing www.bcs.org/ecdl.

The material contained in this courseware publication has not been reviewed for technical accuracy and does not guarantee that candidates will pass the test for the ECDL Certification Programme.

Any and all assessment items and/or performance-based exercises contained in this courseware relate solely to this publication and do not constitute or imply certification by BCS or ECDL Foundation in respect of the ECDL Certification Programme or any other ECDL test.

Irrespective of how the material contained in this courseware is deployed, for example in a learning management system (LMS) or a customised interface, nothing should suggest to the candidate that this material constitutes certification or can lead to certification through any other process than official ECDL certification testing.

For details on sitting a test for an ECDL certification programme in the UK, please visit the BCS website at www.bcs.org/ecdl.

Learners using this courseware must be registered with BCS before undertaking a test for ECDL. Without a valid registration, the test(s) cannot be undertaken and no certificate, nor any other form of recognition, can be given to a learner. Registration should be undertaken with BCS at an Approved Centre.

Software and data files

Microsoft Word 2010 is part of the *Microsoft Office* suite of applications. This guide assumes that the program has been fully installed on your computer. Some features described in this guide may not work correctly if the program was not fully installed.

Downloadable data accompanying this guide contains files to enable the user to practise new techniques without the need for data entry. Newly created files can be saved to the same location.

Downloading the Data Files

The data files associated with this guide must be downloaded from our website. To do this, go to **www.ciatraining.co.uk/data** and follow the simple on-screen instructions.

Your *FastCode* for this guide's data is: **ITQ150**

The data will be installed to the following location in your **Documents** library\folder:

DATA FILES \ Level 1 ITQ \ Word 2010

If you prefer, the data files can also be supplied on CD at an additional cost. Contact the Sales team at info@ciatraining.co.uk.

Overview of the unit

The level 1 unit is called **Word Processing Software** and requires you to use a software application to create and edit text based documents.

At this level, you are expected to select and use a range of basic word processing tools and techniques to produce simple documents.

This guide is designed to be used with *Microsoft Word 2010* and contains exercises covering the following topics:

- Opening, Closing & Saving
- Formatting Text
- Creating Documents
- Entering & Editing Data
- Using Templates
- Checking & Proof Reading
- Printing & Previewing

- Headers & Footers
- Page Setup & Layout
- Alignment & Indentation
- Bullets & Numbering
- Search & Replace
- Creating Tables
- Inserting Art & Pictures

Skill Check

After you have finished working through each Skill Set, come back to this checklist and review your progress. You judge when you are competent – only when you fully understand the learning aims of each exercise topic should you progress to the next Skill Set.

1: No Knowledge **2**: Some Knowledge **3**: Competent

Skill Set	No	Exercise	1	2	3
1 First Steps with Word	1	Understanding Word Processing			
	2	Starting Word			
	3	The Screen Layout			
	4	The Ribbon			
	5	Opening a Document			
	6	Closing a Document			
	7	Starting a New Document			
	8	Closing Word			
2 Creating Documents	10	Input Devices			
	11	Introduction to the Keyboard			
	12	Creating a Document			
	13	Saving a New Document			
	14	Saving a Named Document			
	15	Moving the Cursor			
	16	Using the Mouse			
	17	Inserting Text			
	18	Using Templates			
	19	Completing a Form			
3 Editing Text	21	Deleting Text			
	22	Selecting Words and Sentences			
	23	Selecting Lines and Paragraphs			
	24	Cut, Copy and Paste			
	25	Using Drag and Drop			
	26	Find and Replace			

1: No Knowledge **2**: Some Knowledge **3**: Competent

Skill Set	No	Exercise	1	2	3
4 Formatting Text	28	Underline, Bold and Italic			
	29	Fonts			
	30	Changing Text Size			
	31	Changing Text Colour			
	32	Applying Borders and Shading			
	33	Applying Heading Styles			
5 Formatting Paragraphs	35	Line and Paragraph Spacing			
	36	Alignment			
	37	Indentation			
	38	Applying Bullets and Numbers			
6 Printing	40	Previewing Documents			
	41	Page Orientation			
	42	Changing Paper Size			
	43	Margins			
	44	Headers and Footers			
	45	Page and Paragraph Breaks			
	46	Printing Documents			
7 Creating Tables	48	Tables			
	49	Entering text			
	50	Inserting & Deleting Rows & Columns			
	51	Adjusting Column Width			
	52	Deleting a Table			
8 Inserting Art and Pictures	54	Inserting Clip Art			
	55	Inserting a Picture from File			
	56	Working with Pictures			
	57	Cropping Pictures			
	58	Using Shapes			
9 Checking Your Document	60	Automatic Spell Checking			
	61	Spell Checker			
	62	Grammar Checker			
	63	Proof Reading			

Contents

Skill Set 1

First Steps with Word

By the end of this Skill Set you should be able to:

Understand the Uses of Word Processed Documents

Start *Word*

Recognise the Screen Layout

Use the Ribbon

Open and Close Documents

Find Documents

Start a New Document

Close *Word*

Exercise 1 - Understanding Word Processing

Knowledge:

One of the most widely used applications on computers is word processing. This book uses one of the most popular word processing applications, *Microsoft Word*.

Word processing software such as *Microsoft Word* enables you to produce professional looking, well styled documents for many different purposes. You can create reports, business and personal letters, newsletters, flyers and posters. *Word* even lets you design and create web pages - in fact any *Word* document can be saved in a format that can be viewed on the web.

Word Processed documents can include paragraphs of text, numbers, either in a list or in a table and pictures, or other images. Other elements, such as borders and shading, allow paragraphs, tables and pictures to stand out and make the overall document more interesting.

If you are going to be using a similar type of document time after time, you can create a **template**. This is a document that has specific set features, which you can use as a starting point from which to create many new documents - each of which has the same style.

Before creating a document, it's important to think about who will be reading it. The information you produce should be fit for purpose, i.e. it should put its message across clearly and accurately, and it should be at the right level for its intended audience. For example, you would need to take a different approach when creating a newsletter for children, than when you are producing a formal business report.

You will also need to think about whether the document will be viewed on screen, or whether you will need to print out a hard copy.

Activity:

1. Think about what types of document you could produce for your own use - whether for work, for your studies, or for personal use.

2. Consider the different approaches you could use.

Exercise 2 - Starting Word

Knowledge:

There are a few different ways to start the program. There may be a shortcut on the **Desktop**, or in the **Start** menu; if not you can start it via the usual menus.

Activity:

1. Click once on the **Start** button, 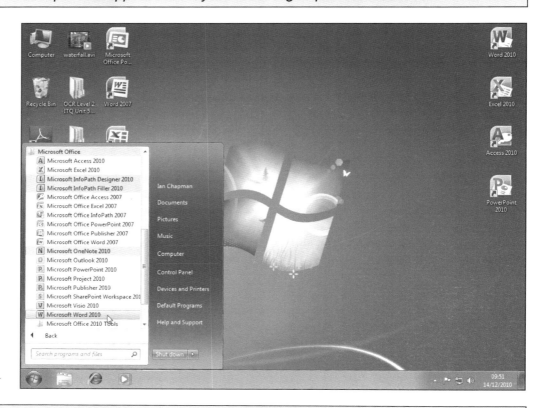, to show the list of start options available. Nearly all *Windows* programs can be started from here.

2. Move the mouse pointer over **All Programs**. After a moment, a full list of programs will be displayed.

3. Click once on the **Microsoft Office** folder to display its contents.

4. To start *Word 2010*, click |W| Microsoft Word 2010 .

> **Note:** There may be slight differences depending on individual installations and set-ups. The application may have been grouped elsewhere.

> **Note:** The listing under **All Programs** and the list at the left of the **Start** menu will be different depending on the software currently installed on the PC.

Exercise 3 - The Screen Layout

Knowledge:

In previous versions of *Microsoft Office* applications, commands were controlled by a series of menus and toolbars. *Word 2010* has replaced these with a **Ribbon** which is displayed at the top of the application window.

Above the **Ribbon** is the **Quick Access Toolbar** which contains a few popular command buttons. By default this toolbar has three buttons, **Save**, **Undo** and **Repeat**. This toolbar can be customised by adding further buttons. When *Word* starts, the following screen appears:

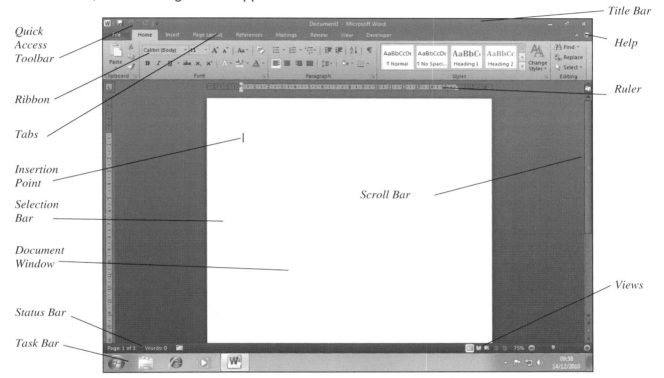

The pictures shown in this guide have used the Black colour scheme for easier viewing

Activity:

1. Look at the top line, the **Title Bar**, displaying **Microsoft Word**. It also shows the title of the current document.

2. Below that is the **Ribbon**, where commands are chosen using the mouse. It is made up of **Tabs** (the words at the top of the ribbon, which illuminate when the mouse is rolled over them), **Groups** (the boxes which spread horizontally across the ribbon, distinguishable by their names at the bottom of each) and **Commands** (the buttons within groups which perform different actions).

3. Find the bar at the bottom of the screen. This is called the **Status Bar**, where the page number will be displayed.

4. The main part of the screen shows a blank document. The default view, shown here is **Print Layout** view.

Exercise 4 - The Ribbon

Knowledge:

The **Ribbon** contains buttons and drop down lists to control the operation of *Word*. The **Ribbon** is divided into a series of **Tabs**, each one of which has a set of controls specific to a certain function or process. On each tab, the controls are further divided into separate **Groups** of connected functions.

Some tabs can be selected manually, some only appear when certain operations are active, for example only when a picture is active, will **Picture Tools** tabs be displayed on the **Ribbon**.

Activity:

1.   On the **Ribbon**, the **Home** tab should be selected. Other basic tabs are available.

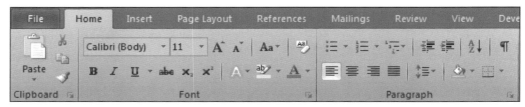

Part of the Ribbon displaying the Home tab

> **Note:**   Any buttons displayed in pale grey are called **ghosted** and are not available to be selected at present.

2.   Notice how the buttons on the **Ribbon** are divided into **Groups** (**Clipboard**, **Font**, **Paragraph**, etc.).

> **Note:**   The display of buttons on the **Ribbon** is dynamic. That is it will change according to how much space there is available. If the window is not maximised or the screen resolution is anything other than 1024 by 768, the **Ribbon** will not always appear as shown in this guide.

3.   Leave the cursor over any the buttons. A **ToolTip** appears which gives more information and an alternative key press for the function, if available.

4.   Some buttons produce immediate effects, like the **Bold**, **Italic** and **Underline** buttons in the **Font** group, used for formatting (changing how the text looks).

5.   Buttons with a drop down arrow, e.g. [Select ▾], lead to further options. Click the **Select** button, which is found in the **Editing** group. A list of further options is displayed. Click on the white page area to close the menu.

> **Note:**   Sometimes it is necessary to click on the drop down arrow itself rather than the rest of the button to get the list of options.

Exercise 4 - Continued

6.   Some options will display a dialog box which needs data to be entered. Click the **Replace** button, the **Find and Replace** dialog box is displayed. Click the **Cancel** button in the dialog box to remove it.

7.   Some groups have a dialog box launcher to the right of the group name, e.g. the **Font** group,

8.   Click the **Font** dialog box launcher to display the **Font** dialog box.

9.   This is a tabbed dialog box that does all font formatting in one place. Click **Cancel** to close the **Font** dialog box.

10. Display the other basic tabs, one at a time, **Insert**, **Page Layout**, **References**, **Mailings**, **Review** and **View** to see which other commands are available.

11. Select the **Home** tab again.

12. Locate the **Quick Access Toolbar**. Point at each button and read its **ToolTip**.

13. The third button is the **Repeat** button. This button changes to a **Redo** button after the **Undo** button has been used.

Exercise 5 - Opening a Document

Knowledge:

Any document saved on disk can be opened from within *Word*. You can also open a file without having the software open; if you do this *Word* will start automatically.

Activity:

1. A screen showing a new blank document should be displayed; this always happens when you start the program.

2. Now you're going to find and open one of the data files supplied with this book. Click the **File** tab to display a menu of main tasks.

3. Click Open,   , to display the **Open** dialog box.

4. Double click on **DATA FILES** on the right to expand the folder.

5. Double click on **Level 1 ITQ**, then **Word 2010** to display the files in the **Word 2010** folder (which should be shown in the **Address Bar**).

Exercise 5 – Continued

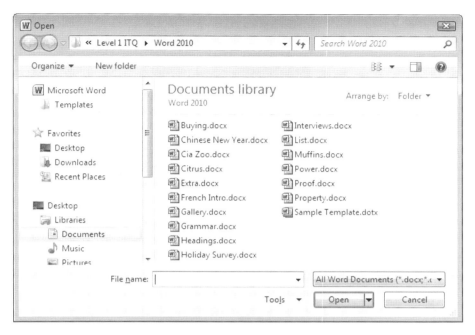

6.   The files are shown in **List** view. The way the files are shown can be changed using **Change your view** button, 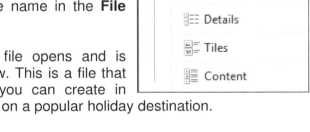.

7.   Choose **Details** to see more information about each file.

8.   Use the **Change your view** button to see some of the other available views, before changing back to **List** view.

9.   Click on **French Intro** from the list of files. This selects the file and places the name in the **File name** box.

10. Click the **Open** button. The file opens and is placed in the document window. This is a file that shows an example of what you can create in *Word*. It's an informative report on a popular holiday destination.

11. Leave the document open.

Note: The keypress *<Ctrl O>* will also open the Open dialog box.

Note: By default, when no document is open clicking on the **File** tab will display the **Recent** screen. This is a list of recently opened documents and recently visited locations that can be used to quickly locate a file.

Exercise 6 - Closing a Document

Knowledge:

Although it's possible to have many documents open at the same time, it's usually more efficient to close a document after you've finished using it. Closing a document doesn't mean that you have to close the application too.

Activity:

1. The document **French Intro** is open from the previous exercise.

2. Click the **File** tab and select **Close** to close the document.

3. If the box below appears, click **Don't Save** to close the document <u>without</u> saving the changes.

4. The screen now appears blank until another, or a new document, is opened.

5.

Note:	*The keypress <Ctrl W> will also close the document.*

Exercise 7 - Starting a New Document

Knowledge:

A new document can be started at any time, whether other documents are open or not. New, blank documents are based on the **Normal** template.

Activity:

1. Click the **File** tab and, from the menu, select **New,** .

2. The **New Document** screen opens.

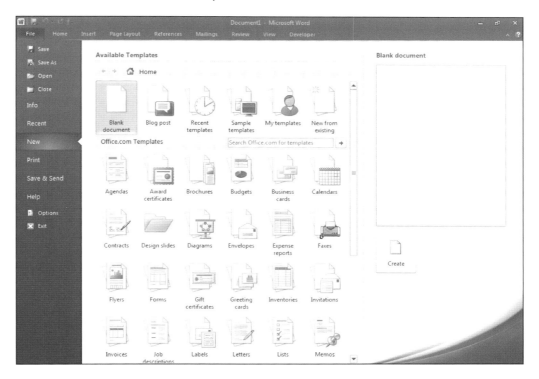

3. The default (most usual) option shows **Home** under **Available Templates** with **Blank document** already selected. The preview on the right shows whatever is selected.

4. Leave the selections as they are and click on **Create** .

5. A new, blank document opens ready for text entry.

6. Close the document <u>without</u> saving any changes.

Exercise 8 - Closing Word

Knowledge:

When *Word* is closed, if any documents are still open and have not been saved, a warning will be displayed with an option to save the changes. This means that you won't lose your work when you close *Word*, if you have forgotten to save it.

Activity:

1. Click the **File** tab to reveal the options.

2. Click the 【**✕ Exit**】 button and *Word* closes down. The **Desktop** is displayed.

> **Note:** *Word can also be closed by clicking the **Close** button, ✕ , in the top right corner of the screen.*

3. Start *Word* again, referring to Exercise 2 if necessary.

Exercise 9 - Develop Your Skills

Note: *This training, which has been approved by BCS, includes exercise items intended to assist learners in their training for a BCS or ECDL Certification Programme. These exercises are not certification tests. For information about how to take a certification test and to find Approved Centres in the UK, please refer to the BCS website at www.bcs.org/qualifications.*

You will find a *Develop Your Skills* exercise at the end of each Skill Set. Work through it to ensure you've understood the previous exercises.

1. What should you think about <u>before</u> creating a new document?

2. Use the mouse pointer to find the **Tooltips** for the following buttons located on the **Home** tab. Read their descriptions:

    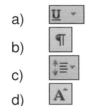

    a)

    b)

    c)

    d)

3. Click on the **View** tab. How many groups are there?

4. The **Review** tab has seven groups; **Comments**, **Changes**, **Proofing**, **Protect**, **Language**, **Tracking** and which other?

5. Open the document **Interviews** from the **Word 2010** folder.

6. Close the document.

7. Close *Word*.

8. Start *Word* again.

Note: *The answers are listed in the **Answers** section at the end of this guide.*

Summary: First Steps with Word

In this Skill Set you have started *Word* and become familiar with the screen layout and the **Ribbon**. You have also opened and closed documents and closed down *Word*.

<u>You should be able to demonstrate your ability to:</u>

- Briefly describe the types of information within a particular document

- Retrieve document files effectively, in line with local guidelines and conventions where available:
    - Find a document
    - Open a document
    - Close a document

Skill Set 2

Creating Documents

By the end of this Skill Set you should be able to:

Understand Input Devices

Recognise Different Parts of the Keyboard

Create a Document

Save a New Document

Save a Named Document

Use the Cursor Keys and Mouse to Move

Insert Text

Use Templates

Complete a Form

Exercise 10 - Input Devices

Knowledge:

Any implement or device used to enter information into a computer is called an **input device**.

The most common is the **keyboard** and information or data is entered by pressing keys. It is commonly used alongside a **mouse** which is used for selecting items. The keyboard will be explored more in the next exercise.

Many of you will have used other input devices without necessarily realising it. Some small gaming devices use a **stylus** to enter or select data. These are also sometimes used with mobile phones.

Instead of a keyboard, some computers, such as the Apple® Ipad, use a **touchscreen** method of input. The keyboard may be displayed on the screen for simple text entry, but other selections are made simply by touching the appropriate part of the screen. Other examples are gaming devices, mobile phones and satellite navigation systems

Voice recognition software is another method of input. This works alongside your usual software, but instead of using the keyboard or mouse, you simple tell the computer what to do. This is useful for some people with disabilities, or for those who need to be using their hands for something else while dictating, e.g. radiographers or pathologists. This has the disadvantage of having to be set up to recognise the user, who must then speak clearly and would not be of much use in a noisy office.

Activity:

1.   What input devices have you used?

Exercise 11 - Introduction to the Keyboard

Knowledge:

You will use the keyboard (*see example below*) a lot when you are word processing. The keyboard (*1*) is basically the same as a typewriter keyboard has always been but there are extra keys. The top row contains the **Function Keys**: <**F1**> to <**F12**> (*3*). These keys are used to access shortcuts in some programs. On the main keyboard, the additional keys used most often are <**Ctrl**>, <**Alt**> (left and right of *11*) and <**Enter**> (*9*) is used for starting a new line.

At the far right of the keyboard is a numeric keypad (*6*), which also includes mathematical keys (+, -, etc.). Numbers can be entered more quickly using these keys. The **Number Lock** must be on to use this keypad - use the top left button on the numeric keypad (<**Num Lock**>) to switch it on or off.

To the left of the numeric keypad are directional keys, such as <**Home**>, <**Page Up**> (*15*) and arrow keys (*7*) that allow movement around a text document, for example. The <**Delete**> (*15*) and <**Backspace**> (*14*) keys are both used to delete text.

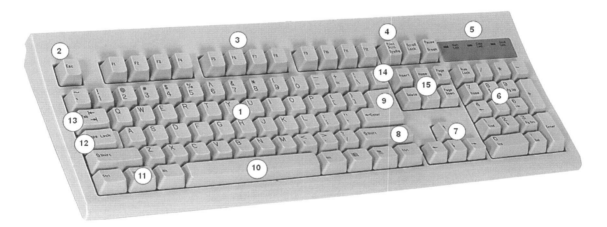

Keys on the diagram not already mentioned are: <**Esc**> (*2*) - the escape key, often an alternative to a **Cancel** option, <**Print Screen**> (*4*) - copies the exact content shown on screen, <**Shift**> (*8*) - hold this down to type a capital letter, or a symbol above another (e.g. £ above the <**3**>). The <**Spacebar**> (*10*) adds one space to text, <**Caps Lock**> (*12*) switches to capitals until pressed again and <**Tab**> (*13*) moves along the page to the next tab stop, set at regular intervals to help line up text. The indicator lights (*5*) show if any locks are activated, such as <**Caps Lock**>.

Activity:

1.   Find each of the numbered areas shown on the diagram above on your own keyboard.

Exercise 12 - Creating a Document

Knowledge:

The keyboard is called an **input device** because it is used to input information to the computer. In a word processing application, any letter, number or symbol typed in is called a **character**.

The cursor can be moved by clicking the mouse pointer or by using the arrow keys on the keyboard. You will practise this in the following exercises. Word processors have a feature called **word wrap**, which means that as you type, when the edge of the paper is reached, the text automatically wraps to the next line. It's just another feature that helps you to work more efficiently.

Activity:

1. A blank document is open.

2. Enter the following text. Type <u>carefully</u> and <u>accurately</u> to try and avoid any mistakes. Remember to use the <**Shift**> key with the letter to make it a capital:

    Shakespeare Removals

3. This is the title. Press <**Enter**> to end the line and start a new paragraph.

4. Continue typing the following paragraph and *Word* will automatically move to the next line when the margins are reached. This is called **word wrap**.

    With over 25 years' experience in the removals business, Shakespeare can give our customers confidence in our professional service. Each removal is different and we treat each one as an individual case.

5. Press <**Enter**>. Type in the following two paragraphs, pressing <**Enter**> in the correct place.

    Local, long distance and international moves undertaken.
    For further information, telephone 0123 4567891.

6. Your document should look like the one below;

    Shakespeare Removals

    With over 25 years' experience in the removals business, Shakespeare can give our customers' confidence in our professional service. Each removal is different and we treat each one as an individual case.

    Local, long distance and International moves undertaken.

    For further information, telephone 0123 4567891.

7. Leave the document open for the next exercise.

Exercise 13 - Saving a New Document

Knowledge:

A file must be saved if it is to be used again. There are two main ways to save, depending on whether the file has been newly created, or whether it has previously been saved and given a name.

A previously saved document can be saved with a different name, to create a new version of the original, without affecting it. You may need to do this if you want to create a new document using the original version as a starting point, but not lose the original.

Once a file has been named, it is important that you are able to locate it again. With this in mind, make sure that the file names you use make sense to you and that you save them to a location that you know and can easily remember. It is important to follow the guidelines and conventions used by your company for naming and storing files. Using random names and storing the files anywhere is a recipe for chaos when someone else needs to find them!

Activity:

1. The document just typed in the previous exercise is still on the screen and needs to be saved.

2. Click the **File** tab and choose the **Save As** command. The **Save As** dialog box will appear. Make sure the **Address Bar** shows the location of the supplied word processing data files.

> **Note:** *If the data folder is not shown, use the note on page 4 to locate them.*

3. The document must be given a name. Use the keyboard to enter **removal** in the **File name** box (the highlighted text will automatically be deleted and the extension **.docx** will be added after saving).

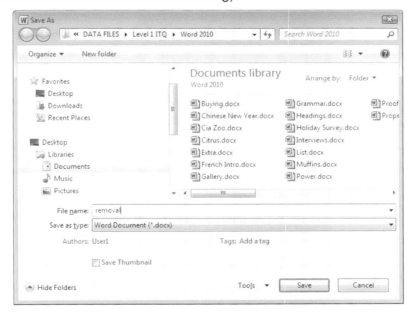

Exercise 13 - Continued

> **Note:** *A file name can be of any length. Choose a meaningful name but do not use any of the following characters: ><"*?:\ /;|.*

4. Click the **Save** button, 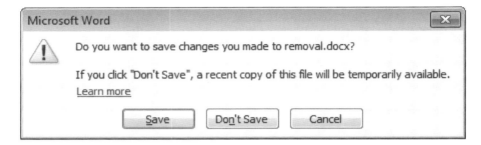, at the bottom right of the dialog box. The chosen name now appears in the **Title Bar**.

5. Press <**Enter**> to start a new paragraph.

6. Type in the name **Mr Shakespeare**.

7. The document has been changed and must either be saved with the same name, saved with a new name or closed without saving the new text. Select the **File** tab and then **Close** from the menu.

8. A dialog box appears, giving you the option of **Save**, saving with the same name, **Don't Save**, closes without saving any changes, or **Cancel** which will return to the document. Select **Don't Save** and the document closes <u>without</u> saving any changes.

> **Note:** *The keypress <**Ctrl S**> will also Save the document.*

Exercise 14 - Saving a Named Document

Knowledge:

Once a document has been saved and, therefore, given a name, it can be updated and saved using the **Save** command. This will keep the same file name and overwrite the previous version.

If an updated document is to be saved, but the original also needs to be kept, then the **Save as** command is used.

Activity:

> **Note:** *A previously named document can be saved to the same location under the same name by clicking the **Save** button,* ▉*, on the **Quick Access Toolbar**. When a new document is to be saved, selecting **Save** also displays the **Save As** dialog box.*

1.   Open the document **removal**.

2.   The cursor appears at the beginning of the document. Type in your name and press <**Enter**>.

3.   Now this file is to be saved with the same name, overwriting the original. Click the **File** tab and choose the **Save** command. The file is saved with the updated text. Close it and open it again to be sure.

4.   With the cursor at the beginning of the document again, enter the text **Typed by:** followed by a space.

5.   This time select **Save As** from the **File** tab. The **Save As** dialog box appears. The diagram in the previous exercise shows an example of how it may look.

6.   Notice that the file name is highlighted in blue. The name of the file (document) can now be changed. Type in **amended**. The highlighted text will be replaced.

> **Note:** *A new folder for your work can be created from this dialog box. If you ever want to do this, click the **New folder** button,* | New folder |*, at the top of the dialog box. Name the folder and press <**Enter**>.*

7.   Check that the **Address Bar** displays the correct location for your data files.

8.   Click the **Save** button, | Save |, at the bottom right of the dialog box. The chosen name, **amended**, now appears in the **Title Bar** at the top of the screen.

9.   Close the document.

Exercise 15 - Moving the Cursor

Knowledge:

The cursor keys can be used to move the cursor character by character and line by line. Some of the more useful movement keys are as follows:

Description	Key Press	Description	Key Press
Beginning of a line	<Home>	Beginning of next paragraph	<Ctrl ↓>
End of a line	<End>	Up one paragraph	<Ctrl ↑>
Beginning of document	<Ctrl Home>	Next word	<Ctrl →>
End of a document	<Ctrl End>	Previous word	<Ctrl ←>
Next page	<Ctrl Page Down>	Previous page	<Ctrl Page Up>

> **Note:** An efficient way to move the cursor around the screen is to position the mouse and click the left button.

Where two keys are mentioned, hold down the first key, while pressing and releasing the second.

Activity:

1. Click the **File** tab and then **Open**. To open the document **Property**, as an alternative to click and **Open**, double click on the file name.

2. Position the cursor in the middle of the title and then press <**End**> the cursor moves to the end of the line.

3. Move down a paragraph using <**Ctrl ↓**>. Remember every time you press the <**Enter**> key a new paragraph is formed. Try <**Ctrl ↓**> again to move to the beginning of the next paragraph.

4. Move to the end of the document using <**Ctrl End**>.

5. Move to the beginning of the document using <**Ctrl Home**>.

6. Press <**Ctrl →**> to move to the beginning of the next word. Continue using this key press until you are on the next line.

7. Press <**Ctrl Page Down**> to move to the beginning of the second page.

> **Note:** The key presses <**Page Up**> and <**Page Down**> moves to the next screen up or down.

8. Use a key press to return to the beginning of the document.

9. Leave the document open.

Exercise 16 - Using the Mouse

Knowledge:

The mouse provides an efficient way of moving around a document. Although small movements are normally made using the keyboard, the mouse and scroll bars are used to move to a different area. To move to a particular place on the document, simply point and click. The usual method of moving around the screen is by a combination of key presses and mouse movements.

Activity:

1. The document **Property** should still be open, if not open it.

2. This is a two page document; check the **Status Bar** to confirm this.

Page: 1 of 2 | Words: 564

3. Scroll bar arrows can be used to move around a document from left to right or up and down.

4. Click once on the down arrow at the right edge of the document to scroll down the document by a small amount.

5. Click once on the up arrow at the right edge of the document to move the document up by a small amount.

6. Click on the scroll button and while holding the mouse button down, drag the button to the bottom of the scroll bar.

Page: 1
A Home Abroad

Note: This view is called **Print Layout** and shows how text, graphics and other parts of a document are placed on the page when it is printed.

Note that the page number and title of the document is shown in a tooltip. As the scroll button is moved down to reveal the second page, the tooltip displays **Page: 2**.

Exercise 16 - Continued

7. Click in the scroll bar above the button to move up the screen. If you need to, continue clicking above the button until the top of the document is in view.

8. Experiment with the scroll bar, scroll buttons and scroll arrows.

9. Use <**Ctrl Home**> to redisplay the beginning of the document with the cursor in front of the title.

10. Move the cursor, I, to the end of the first paragraph after **a later stage**. Click once and the insertion point now flashes where you clicked. Text could now be entered here.

11. Practise moving the cursor around the screen. You can even click in the middle of words.

12. Close the document **Property** <u>without</u> saving.

Exercise 17 - Inserting Text

Knowledge:

Once text has been entered it is a simple task to add more at the end or, indeed, in the middle of it. The insertion point, as the name implies, is the point where text is inserted. Click with the mouse button to place the insertion point in the correct place.

Activity:

1. Open the document **amended** (saved earlier).

2. At the end of the document enter the text **Mr Shakespeare**.

3. Place the insertion point before **Shakespeare** by moving the mouse pointer into position and clicking.

Mr Shakespeare   Mr Shakespeare

Insertion point in position   *After clicking the mouse button*

4. Enter the text **William** followed by a space.

5. Place the insertion point at the end of the document (after **Shakespeare**) and press <**Enter**>.

6. Enter **Stratford** as the address.

7. Place the insertion point in between the two sentences in the longer paragraph. (Before **Each...**)

8. Type in **We specialise in moving pianos and larger musical instruments.**. Notice how the second sentence moves to accommodate the new text. Your document should look similar to that below;

Typed by: Bill Barnacle

Shakespeare Removals

With over 25 years' experience in the removals business, Shakespeare can give our customers' confidence in our professional service. We specialise in moving pianos and larger musical instruments. Each removal is different and we treat each one as an individual case.

Local, long distance and international moves undertaken.

For further information, telephone 0123 4567891.

Mr William Shakespeare

Stratford

---

9. Save the document as **shakespeare** and close it.

Exercise 18 - Using Templates

Knowledge:

All new documents (even blank ones) are based on a template – this is the default template. A template is a style of document that contains standard information, allowing similar documents to be created, e.g. faxes, memos, letters, forms, CVs, etc.

Templates can often help by providing a starting point when you have to create a new document. They usually have suitable headings, with the subject matter to be included in square brackets; these brackets and their contents are replaced with the relevant information. Templates can be really useful in a work environment; you may find that your organisation has created its own set of templates.

Activity:

1. To see the available templates, click the **File** tab and select **New**.

2. Select **Sample templates** from the options at the top of the screen.

Sample templates

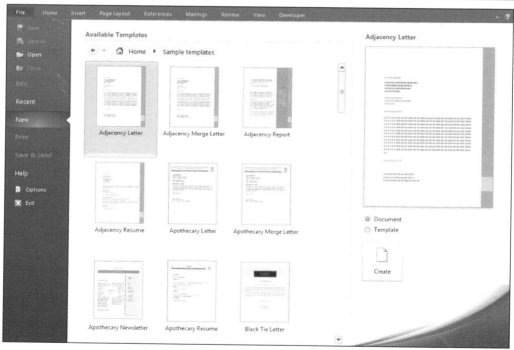

3. A range of installed templates is displayed, with a preview of the one selected on the right. Scroll down and click on the template **Equity Letter**. This is a template that could form the basis of any letter you may want to send. The vital information is included, such as who the letter is from and to whom it is addressed.

> **Note:** To use a template, a document based on a particular template is opened, completed and then saved. The template remains unaffected.

Exercise 18 - Continued

4. Click on **Create** to view the template as a document on screen. Replace the text enclosed in brackets with some 'made up' information, as well as in the main body of the letter. The layout and graphics would be consistent whenever this template was used.

[Pick the date]

Bill Barnacle
[Type the sender company name]
[Type the sender company address]

[Type the recipient name]
[Type the recipient address]

[Type the salutation]

On the Insert tab, the galleries include items that are designed to coordina
You can use these galleries to insert tables, headers, footers, lists, cover pa

5. Save this document as **equity letter** and then close it.

6. Use the **File** tab and **New** to open the **Sample templates** again. Select the **Memos** icon, and look at the preview. It shows a selection of memos ready for completion. Using the template means that no important information will be left out.

7. Click on **Memo (simple design)** then **Create** (or **Download** if it is from Office.com Templates) to open this template as a document. (If you cannot find this Memo, then select any other.)

8. Click in the area **To:** and replace **[Recipient names]** with **Eileen, Bob, George, Claire**. Use the **Tab** key to move to the area **From:** and enter your name.

> *Note:* *Use the earlier keyboard picture to locate the **Tab** key.*

9. Either, click in the areas to be replaced, or press <**Tab**> until the insertion point is in the correct place. Complete the remaining areas by typing in this information:

    CC: Brian

    Date: Select todays date

    Re: Excellent sales results

    Comments: Everyone will be receiving a £1000 bonus this month. Well done.

> *Note:* *Dates in installed templates are in American format, but can be changed.*

10. Save the document as **memo** and then close it.

> *Note:* *There are many more templates available, both from **Sample templates** and from **Office.com Templates**. The latter are shown grouped by type and must be downloaded. An internet connection is required.*

Exercise 19 - Completing a Form

Knowledge:

A form is a kind of template, where only the answer fields can be completed, i.e. you cannot make any changes to the introduction or the questions, because they are protected. The form is completed on screen and can then be saved with a new name or can be printed.

You may encounter computer generated forms when choosing a holiday, applying for road tax or applying for a job.

Activity:

1.   Open the document **Holiday Survey**.

2.   Drop down the list of answers for the first question.

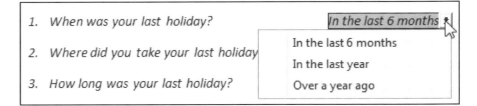

3.   Make a selection, then click in the next answer.

4.   Continue to make selections until question 7. Here click in either the **Yes** or the **No** box.

5.   Question 8 requires a written answer. Click in the box and suggest that the pool could be cleaned more regularly.

6.   Next, drop down the list next to the date request. This is called a **Date Picker** and is used instead of typing in the date. Select any date or click on Today.

7.   Place a cross in the box if you want to be entered in the draw.

8.   Enter the information requested in the last box.

9.   Save the completed form as **my form** and then close it.

Exercise 20 - Develop Your Skills

You will find a *Develop Your Skills* exercise at the end of each Skill Set. Work through it to ensure you've understood the previous exercises.

1. Use the **Oriel Fax** template supplied with *Word,* use the scroll bar to find it. Complete it with the following information, adding your own details where appropriate:

    The fax is to **CiA Training**
    Their fax number is **0191 549 9005** and phone is **0191 549 9005**
    There is **1** page and the subject **(RE:)** of the fax is **Training Materials**.
    The comments are: **Please could you send me training materials for Word 2010 urgently, at introductory and intermediate level?**

2. Save the completed fax cover sheet as **urgent request**.

3. Close the document.

4. Start a new, blank document and type in the following text (ignore any wavy green or red lines under the text):

    The Chipping Wood Sports Complex is the first of its kind to be built in the county. It has facilities to impress even the biggest sports enthusiasts: an Olympic size swimming pool with adjustable depth level, a 250 square metre sports hall, spa area, sauna and hammam and a 150 seater self service restaurant.
    The manager, Bernie Tyzack, is very excited about the opening of the complex next week. "I'm sure such a well equipped centre will bring many new visitors to the town and do wonders for the local economy", he said during a brief interview.

5. Save the document as **sports**.

6. Some facilities have been missed out. Add **squash courts** after **sports hall**. Add **with Jacuzzi** after **spa area**.

7. Save the changes to the document, using the same name.

8. Close the document.

Summary: Creating Documents

In this Skill Set you have studied input devices, created and saved a new document, saved a named document, moved around a document, and added text within a document. You have also become familiar with templates and forms.

<u>You should be able to demonstrate your ability to:</u>

- Recognise standard document layouts:
    - Existing templates
    - Memos, forms, job applications

- Understand templates and when to use them

- Create documents:
    - Enter text and numbers
    - Use the full range of keys
    - Type accurately and efficiently
    - Use keyboard shortcuts
    - Insert text
    - Wrap text

- Be familiar with other input devices:
    - Voice recognition
    - Touch screen
    - Stylus

- Save documents:
    - New document
    - Using a previously saved document, change and save:
        - Named document with same name
        - Named document with a different name

Skill Set 3

Editing Text

By the end of this Skill Set you should be able to:

Delete Text
Select Words and Sentences
Select Lines and Paragraphs
Cut, Copy and Paste Text
Use Drag and Drop
Use Find and Replace

Exercise 21 - Deleting Text

Knowledge:

Both the mouse and the cursor keys can be used to move the insertion point. Mistakes can be deleted. Errors can be undone or redone.

Activity:

1.   Open the document **Muffins**

2.   The cursor will be at the beginning of the document before the word **Blueberry**.

> **Note:** *Characters to the left of the cursor are deleted by pressing the <Backspace> key and characters to the right of the cursor are deleted using the <Delete> key. Use the keyboard picture in the Introduction to the Keyboard exercise to locate the keys.*

3.   Delete **Blue** using the <**Delete**> key.

4.   In its place, type in **Rasp**.

5.   Replace **blueberries** with **raspberries** in the **Ingredients** using the <**Backspace**> key.

6.   Change the other occurrence of **blueberries** using either method.

7.   Change the number of eggs from **2** to **3**.

8.   This is a mistake. Click the **Undo** button [icon] from the **Quick Access Toolbar**. The number changes back.

9.   Actually, no, you were right first time. Click the **Redo** button [icon] and the number changes again.

> **Note:** *Several changes can be undone in one go by clicking the drop down arrow at the side of the Undo button,* [icon].

10.   To save the document with a new name, click the **File** tab and select **Save As**.

11.   In the **File name** box, type **raspberry muffins**. This changes the name of the file to be saved.

12.   Click the **Save** button. The file is saved with the new name. The original file **Muffins** is unaffected.

13.   Close the document.

Exercise 22 - Selecting Words and Sentences

Knowledge:

Most features of *Word* work on the basis that text is first selected and an action is then performed upon the selected text, deleting, for example. There are various ways to select text - use the method you prefer. Once you are able to select text correctly, creating documents will be much quicker.

Activity:

1. Open the document **Buying**.

2. Text can be selected by clicking and dragging the mouse. In the first paragraph, select the final word, **stage** (by clicking at the beginning of the word and, holding down the mouse button, drag to the end of the word before releasing the mouse button).

3. **stage** is highlighted to show that it has been selected. Now delete it by pressing <**Delete**>.

4. It is easier to select a word by double clicking on it. Double click on **later**, which is now the last word in the first paragraph and delete it.

5. Now select the first sentence in the document by clicking and dragging.

6. To remove the text selection, click once, away from the selected text.

> **Note:** Once text is selected, if any key is pressed, the selected text will be deleted and replaced with the key press. Be careful - always remove the selection before pressing keys.

7. An easy way to select a sentence is to hold down the <**Ctrl**> key and click anywhere within the sentence. Select the first sentence of the second paragraph using this method.

8. Delete the selected text.

9. The cursor keys can be used together with the <**Shift**> key to select text. Position the cursor at the beginning of the text.

10. Hold down <**Shift**> and press → several times. This selects the text character by character – this includes spaces.

11. As you know, <**Ctrl** →> moves the cursor word by word, so combined with <**Shift**> it selects word by word.

12. Test this by holding down both <**Shift**> and <**Ctrl**> and using → to make a selection. Click away to remove the selection.

13. Close the document without saving to lose the recent changes.

© *CiA Training Ltd 2013*

Exercise 23 - Selecting Lines and Paragraphs

Knowledge:

The **Selection Bar**, an invisible area at the left margin of the page, is used to select larger areas of text.

Activity:

1. Open the document **Buying** again.

2. Move the mouse pointer towards the left margin until it changes to 𝄃. This is the selection arrow.

3. Move the mouse to the first paragraph, making sure the selection arrow is still visible and click once to select a line of text.

4. Click again, away from the margin, to remove the selection.

5. At the left of the first paragraph, display the selection arrow again. This time, double click the mouse to select the whole paragraph.

6. Remove the selection and display the selection arrow again.

7. Click at the beginning of the first paragraph and, holding down the mouse button, drag to the end of the second paragraph. Two paragraphs are now highlighted.

A Home Abroad

Many people are now relocating to another country, in search of a more relaxed way of life and guaranteed sunshine for at least part of the year. Those who don't want to make a total commitment to a new country may choose to buy a holiday home in the sun, perhaps with a view to retiring there at a later stage.

Before searching for a property abroad, there are some basic questions that you should ask, which should help in making a choice of location:

* Do you speak the language?

8. To select the entire document, click three times in rapid succession, in the **Selection Bar**.

> **Note:** *The key press <Ctrl A> can also be used to select the whole document.*

9. Now press <**Delete**>. The whole document is deleted.

10. Close the document <u>without</u> saving any changes.

Exercise 24 - Cut, Copy and Paste

Knowledge:

The **Cut, Copy** and **Paste** commands allow text to be moved around a document, from one place to another, quickly and easily. When text is cut, it is removed from its original location; when copied, the original remains untouched.

When copied or cut, text is placed in a temporary storage area known as the **Clipboard**. Up to **24** cut or copied items can be held on the **Clipboard**.

Words, lines, paragraphs or whole documents can be copied from elsewhere and pasted into your current document.

Activity:

1. Open the document **List**. This document contains a list of things to do this week. The list is numbered in order of importance. Your task is to re-order the items, so that they appear from 1-10.

2. Make sure the **Clipboard** is visible: if not, click the **Clipboard** launcher.

3. Because the **Clipboard** is shared between all *Office* applications, there may already be some items on it. If so, click the **Clear All** button, .

4. Use any method to highlight the sentence **1) E-mail list of overtime payments to payroll** and click the **Cut** button, . An icon representing the cut text appears on the **Clipboard**.

5. Click at the beginning of the document or press **<Ctrl Home>**.

6. Click the **Paste** button, to place the cut text at the insertion point.

7. Number **2** is now in the correct place, but the rest of the list needs to be sorted. Select the line for number **3**.

8. Cut the text. It is placed on the **Clipboard**, above the first item. Filling the **Clipboard** in this way is known as **Collect and Paste**.

9. Place the cursor in the correct position and click item **3** on the **Clipboard** to paste it.

Note: *To use the keyboard for these commands, place the cursor in the word or select the text as usual, then press <Ctrl X>for **Cut**, <Ctrl C>for **Copy** and <Ctrl V>for **Paste**.*

Exercise 24 - Continued

10. In the same way, re-order the remaining items.

11. Another meeting is to be arranged with the business manager, this time to discuss annual leave for the coming year. Select item **6) Arrange meeting with business manager to discuss recruitment**.

12. The new item is almost the same as number **6**. To save time, click the **Copy** button, 🖻. Notice how the original text is untouched, because you've copied it rather than cut it.

13. Start a new line at the end of the document.

14. Paste the copied item.

15. Change the number **6** to **11**. Change the word **recruitment** to **annual leave**.

> 1) E-mail list of overtime payments to payroll
> 2) Add sales figures for this week to the spreadsheet
> 3) Start quarterly sales report
> 4) Send list of required stationery to admin before the requisition on Friday
> 5) Review bonus payments
> 6) Arrange meeting with business manager to discuss recruitment
> 7) Meet with sales team to discuss next initiative
> 8) Decide on new incentives for sales staff
> 9) Research membership of local business clubs
> 10) Liaise with staff to arrange monthly night out
> 11) Arrange meeting with business manager to discuss annual leave

Note: *To paste all items on the **Clipboard**, place the cursor in the required position and select **Paste All**, 🗐 Paste All.*

16. Delete all items from the **Clipboard** by clicking the **Clear All** button, 🗙 Clear All.

17. Close the **Clipboard** task pane. It will not be available until you open it again.

18. Without closing **List**, open the document **Extra**. This contains some extra items that need to be added to the list.

19. Only the first two are required. Select and copy lines **12** and **13**.

20. Close the document **Extra**, so revealing the original document **List**.

21. Paste in the two new lines at the end of the document

22. Save the document as **ordered** and then close it

Exercise 25 - Using Drag and Drop

Knowledge:

Word has many shortcuts that can be used to help you work more quickly and efficiently. You've just looked at cut, copy and paste, but the **drag and drop** facility speeds up the process of moving text from one location to another within a document. This method of moving text does <u>not</u> place it in the **Clipboard**. It is best used to move small amounts of text, cut and paste works better with larger areas.

Activity:

1.   Open the document **Muffins**. This is a recipe for a magazine, which you have been asked to check.

2.   You think some of the text should be moved. Select the bullet **Stud each muffin with about 8 blueberries** and move the mouse over the text until it becomes an arrow.

3.   Click and hold down the mouse button, then drag the mouse to the beginning of the last bullet. As the text is being dragged, the cursor becomes ⌖ and the **Status Bar** reads **Move to where?**. A vertical line appears where the text will be inserted, as shown below.

> •   Cream the butter and sugar together then slowly add the e(
>   minutes
> •   Add the flour, baking powder, nutmeg, and refrigerate for a
> •   Stud each muffin with about 8 blueberries
> •   Place a spoonful of muffin mixture into each muffin case, fil
>   over half way
> •   Take in an oven set at 200C/400F/Gas 6 for 20 minutes or
>   top.

4.   Release the mouse to drop the text in front of the last bullet.

> **Note:**   *The drag and drop feature becomes drag and copy if the **<Ctrl>** key is held down whilst the text is being dragged. The cursor appears as ⊞ and the **Status Bar** reads **Copy to where?***

5.   Practise moving and copying within this document using the drag and drop technique.

6.   Close the document <u>without</u> saving.

Exercise 26 - Find and Replace

Knowledge:

There may be times when a word or phrase in a document has to be replaced - a change of company name, for example. Visually searching for the word or phrase can take a long time, especially if the document is a lengthy one. *Word* allows you to search for and replace text quickly. The **Find** command displays a specific word or string of characters in the **Navigation** pane. The **Replace** facility gives the option to exchange each occurrence of a particular word, or string of words, with an alternative.

Activity:

1. Open the document **French Intro** and make sure the cursor is at the beginning of the text.

2. On the **Home** tab, click on **Find**. (if you click on the drop down arrow, click on **Find** again.) This displays the **Navigation** pane on the left.

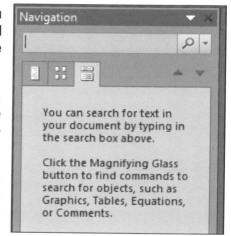

3. The cursor is flashing in the search box, enter **Dordogne**. All occurrences of the word are displayed in the **Navigation** pane and highlighted in the text.

4. Click on the entry that begins **Les Eyzies...**. The document shows page **2** with this entry highlighted in a different colour.

5. Click on the cross next to the search box to clear it ready for the next one.

6. Find all occurrences of the word **cave**. Go to the entry that starts **The famous caves...**.

7. Close the **Navigation** pane using the close button ▣ and return to the beginning of the document.

8. To replace the word **region** with **area**, click ▣ Replace . Enter **region** in the **Find what** box and **area** in **Replace with** box.

Note: *<Ctrl H> will display the **Find and Replace** dialog box with the **Replace** tab selected.*

Exercise 26 - Continued

9. Select **Find Next** and click **Replace**. The search replaces this occurrence and moves on to the next.

> **Note:** **Replace All** *will quickly replace all occurrences of the specified text.*

10. Continue through the document, replacing all occurrences of **region**. When the replacement is complete, one of the following dialog boxes will appear, depending on whether **Replace** or **Replace All** has been selected:

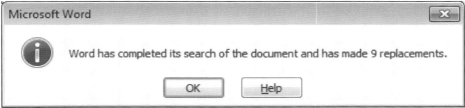

11. Click **OK** then click **Close** to close the **Find and Replace** dialog box.

> **Note:** *To view the **Find and Replace** dialog box more quickly, press **<Ctrl F>**.*

12. Save the document as **french searched** and close it.

Exercise 27 - Develop Your Skills

You will find a *Develop Your Skills* exercise at the end of each Skill Set. Work through it to ensure you've understood the previous exercises.

1. Open the file **Gallery**. Managers at the museum have asked you to make some changes to this promotional literature.

2. Use either cut and paste, or drag and drop, to move the acknowledgement to *Wikipedia* from the bottom of the text and place it at the top.

3. The managers do not want a reference to the damage in this article. Delete the entire paragraph starting **In 1993**.

4. Change **...fell...** in paragraph 2 to **died out**.

5. Save the edited document as **museum**.

6. Type your name and today's date at the bottom of the text, on a new line.

> **Note:** *Depending on how you moved the text in step 2, this text may be italic as you type it in. If so, ignore it for the present.*

7. Save the document as **museum2** and then close it.

8. Open the document **Muffins**.

9. Open the **Find and Replace** dialog box with the **Replace** tab displayed.

10. Replace all occurrences of **Blueberry** with **Raspberry** and **blueberries** with **raspberries**.

11. Save as **muffins2** and close the document.

Summary: Editing Text

In this Skill Set you have selected text (words, sentences, lines, paragraphs, whole documents) and deleted text. You have also learned to use cut, copy, paste, and the drag & drop technique to move and copy text.

<u>You should be able to demonstrate your ability to:</u>

- Select text:
    - Words
    - Sentences
    - Lines
    - Paragraphs
    - Entire document

- Copy and move text using:
    - Cut, copy and paste
    - Drag and drop

- Copy a paragraph from one document to another

- Edit text using:
    - Delete
    - Undo and Redo
    - Find and replace

Skill Set 4

Formatting Text

By the end of this Skill Set you should be able to:

Use Underline, Bold and Italic

Change Fonts and Text Size

Change Text Colour

Apply Borders and Shading

Apply Heading Styles

Exercise 28 - Underline, Bold and Italic

Knowledge:

The **Underline**, **Bold** and **Italic** features allow text to be emphasised, so it stands out on the page. Although text can be formatted as it is typed, a more efficient way is to enter text first, then format it later. All three buttons are found on the **Home** tab in the **Font** group.

Activity:

1.   Open the document **Power**.

2.   Select the title **Solar Energy** and click the **Italic** button, $\boxed{I}$, from the **Font** group. The title is now in italics (sloping to the right).

3.   Now select the paragraph heading **Solar Panels** and click the **Bold** button, $\boxed{B}$.

4.   Make the paragraph headings **Solar Water Heating**, **Photovoltaic (Solar Electricity)** and **Passive Solar Design** bold too.

5.   Underline the first paragraph, below the title, using the **Underline** button, $\boxed{U}$.

6.   The last paragraph is to have all three effects added to it. Select the paragraph.

7.   Click the **Bold** button and then the **Italic** button. To apply a different underline, click the drop down arrow at the right of the button and choose the **Dotted underline** option.

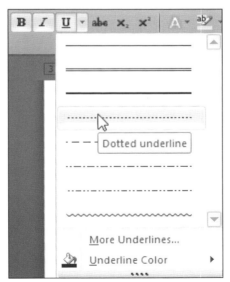

8.   Leave the document open for the next exercise.

Note: *To use the keyboard for these commands, place the cursor in the word or select the text as usual, then press <Ctrl B> for **Bold**, <Ctrl I> for **Italics** and <Ctrl U> for **Underline**.*

Exercise 29 - Fonts

Knowledge:

A font is a type or style of text. There are two different types of font: **serif** and **sans serif**. A serif font, e.g. Times New Roman, Book Antiqua, has extra lines or curls on the 'stalk' of the letters (q); a sans serif font, e.g. Arial, Comic Sans MS, Tahoma, does not (**q**). A combination of the software in use and the selected printer determines which fonts are available for use.

> **Note:** To change the font of a single word, position the cursor within the word and choose the required font.

Activity:

1.   Use the **Power** document. Select the whole of the document.

2.   The quickest way to change a font is via the **Font** box. This is found on the **Home** tab, in the **Font** group. Click the drop down arrow at the right of the box to display the list of available fonts.

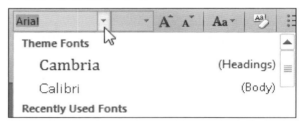

3.   Notice when you drop the list down, how the name of the font is displayed in that font to give you an idea of how your text will look. The text in your document also has a preview of the font applied.

4.   Scroll through the list and select **Garamond**.

> **Note:** If any of these fonts are unavailable, then select an alternative.

5.   Select the first paragraph.

6.   Use the **Font** box to change the font of this paragraph to **Calibri**.

7.   Close the document <u>without</u> saving.

> **Note:** If there is a long list of fonts and you know which one you want to use, drop down the list and start to type in the name of the required font. The font will be displayed for selection.

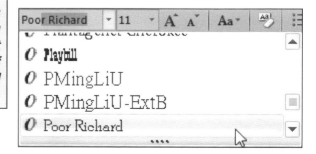

Exercise 30 - Changing Text Size

Knowledge:

The size of printed text can be changed either before or after the text is typed. The range of sizes available will be determined by a combination of the printer, software and font in use. Size is defined in **points** (pt) - the larger the point size, the larger the character appears.

Activity:

1. Open the document **Gallery**.

2. Select the first sentence.

3. Click the drop down arrow at the right of the **Font Size** box, to display a list of sizes. It is found on the **Home** tab, in the **Font** group.

4. Select size **12pt** and the size of the selected text increases.

5. Place the cursor within the word **Medici** in the second sentence and change its size to **16pt**. Remember single words do not have to be selected to be changed.

6. Increase the size of **"uffizi"** in the same sentence to **20pt**.

> The Uffizi Gallery is a palace in Florence, Italy, containing one of the oldest and most famous art museums in the world. Building of the palace was begun by Giorgio Vasari in 1560 for Cosimo I de' Medici as the offices for the Florentine magistrates ("uffizi" means "offices"). Building ended in 1581. The internal courtyard is long and narrow, and open to the river Arno at its far end through a screen. Vasari, a painter as well as architect, emphasized the perspective length by the matching the cornices of all of the roofs.

7. Select the final sentence of the document and change it to **48pt**. You may have to use the scroll bar at the right side of the size list to reach 48.

8. Select the whole document.

9. Use the **Font Size** box to change the text to **16pt** and the font to **Arial**.

10. Click in front of the first word of the document then change the **Font Size** to **20pt**. Type **Gallery** and press <**Enter**>. The word will be formatted with the new size.

11. Save the document as **gallery2** and close it.

Exercise 31 - Changing Text Colour

Knowledge:

Colour can be applied to text, making it more eye-catching. Subtle use of colour can be used to draw attention to certain areas of a document.

Activity:

1.   Open the document **Citrus**.

2.   Select the title then click the drop down arrow on the **Font Color** button. This is found on the **Home** tab, in the **Font** group.

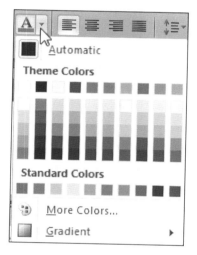

3.   Click on a shade of orange to change the colour of the title.

4.   Change the colour of **greenhouse** in paragraph 1 to green, using the **Font Color** button.

5.   Use the **Font Color** button to make the following changes:

   any mention of **citrus** - orange
   any reference to **sun/sunny/sunlight** - yellow
   any reference to **water** - blue
   last paragraph: **greenfly** - green
   and **red spider mite** - red.

6.   Save the amended document as **colourful**.

7.   Close the document.

Exercise 32 - Applying Borders and Shading

Knowledge:

Borders can be created around text to add interest, or applied to the whole page as a finishing touch. Shading can also be added to specific areas of text or paragraphs for emphasis.

Activity:

1. Open the document **Power**. Click anywhere in the paragraph about Solar Panels.

2. Click the drop down arrow on the **Border** button, 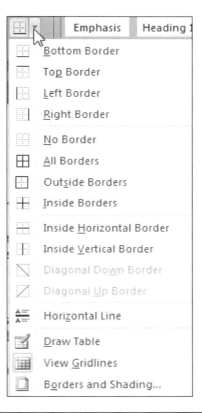, in the **Paragraph** group.

Note:	Your **Borders** button may look different, as it always changes to the last used button.

3. Select **Outside Borders**. A line border should now surround the whole paragraph.

4. To remove the border, display the drop down list again and select **No Border** remembering to have the cursor inside the paragraph.

5. Place the cursor in the paragraph about **Solar Water Heating**. This time, from the list, select **Bottom Border**, display the list a second time and select **Top Border**. This applies a border to the top and bottom of the text only.

Exercise 32 - Continued

6. To remove the top border only, display the **Borders** list and click the **Top Border** button again.

7. Click on the **Page Layout** tab. Locate the **Page Background** group and click on **Page Borders**.

8. The **Borders and Shading** dialog box opens at the **Page Border** tab.

9. Select a **Box** border from the **Setting** area and click **OK**. Notice the difference between this page border, which surrounds the whole page and the previous border which surrounds the content only.

> **Note:** If a document has several pages, a page border will be applied to all of them.

10. Close the document <u>without</u> saving.

11. Open the document **Buying**.

12. To make the last paragraph stand out, it can be shaded. Click anywhere in the paragraph immediately under the **Helping you through the process** heading.

13. Click the **Home** tab and drop down the **Shading** list from the **Paragraph** group.

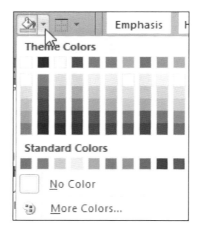

14. Choose a shade of grey from the first column of **Theme Colors**.

15. Shade the other paragraphs as you wish, but making sure the text is visible through the colour.

16. Save the document as **buying2** and close it.

Exercise 33 - Applying Heading Styles

Knowledge:

A style is a predefined list of characteristics that can be applied to text. This could include the **font**, **size**, whether it was **underlined** or not, had **borders** and **shading**, etc. Once a style has been defined it can be applied to text. This means that similar areas of text, such as a heading, will all have exactly the same characteristics. For example, the Exercise titles in this book all have the same style applied.

Word has some styles already defined that can be applied to any document.

Activity:

1.   Open the document **Headings**.

2.   Click on the title. Look at the **Styles** group on the **Home** tab. The **Normal** style has a yellow box around it showing that this text has the **Normal** style applied.

3.   With the cursor still within the title, click on **Heading 1** in the **Styles** group. The text changes to a larger blue font.

4.   Select the next title **Solar Panels**. Click on the drop down arrow (**More**) in the **Styles** group.

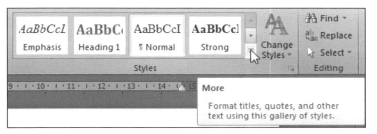

5.   Select **Subtitle** from the expanded list.

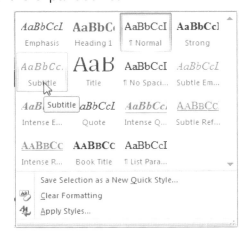

6.   Select the remaining titles in turn and apply the **Subtitle** style to them. Notice that **Subtitle** is displayed in the **Styles** box for ease of use.

7.   Close the document <u>without</u> saving.

Exercise 34 - Develop Your Skills

You will find a *Develop Your Skills* exercise at the end of each Skill Set. Work through it to ensure you've understood the previous exercises.

1.   Open the document **French Intro**.

2.   Change the font of all the text to **Tempus Sans ITC**, including the text in the box.

3.   Change the size of the title to **24pt** and its colour to dark olive green.

4.   Increase the size of the text in the shaded box to **12pt**.

5.   Make the text in the shaded box bold.

6.   In the second paragraph change the colour of **Périgord Vert** to green and **Périgord Pourpre** to purple - any purplish shade will do.

7.   Scroll down to page 2 and change the size of the **History** subheading to **12pt** and its colour to dark olive green.

8.   In the **History** section, make the references to **Julius Caesar**, **Eleanor of Aquitaine** and **Henri Plantagenet** italic.

9.   On page 3, apply a simple box border to the paragraph starting **This history of conflict…**

10.   Shade this paragraph with light olive green.

11.   Change the size of the very last line of text to **72pt**.

12.   Apply **Heading 1** style to the main title **The Dordogne**.

13.   Apply **Heading 2** style to the sub heading **History**.

14.   Save the document as **french amended**.

15.   Close the document.

Summary: Formatting Text

In this Skill Set you have formatted text using bold, underline and italic. You have also changed the font type and font size, applied borders and shading, and applied heading styles to text.

<u>You should be able to demonstrate your ability to:</u>

- Format text:
    - Bold, underline and italic
    - Change font type
    - Change font size
    - Apply borders and shading
    - Apply heading styles

Skill Set 5

Formatting Paragraphs

By the end of this Skill Set you should be able to:

Change Line and Paragraph Spacing
Change Paragraph Alignment
Change Paragraph Indentation
Apply Bullets and Numbering

Exercise 35 - Line and Paragraph Spacing

Knowledge:

The appearance and readability of a document can be improved by changing line spacing. By default, in *Word 2010*, line spacing is **1.15sp**; other commonly used spacing is **double** or **1½**. Spacing before and/or after a paragraph can also be changed. Spacing is measured in **points**: **12pt** is equal to one line for a size 12 font.

Again, to improve readability and display, you can use a control that prevents *Word* from separating the last line of a paragraph and printing it at the top of a new page (widow), or separating the first line of a new paragraph and leaving it at the bottom of the current page (orphan). By default, the **Widows and Orphans** control is on.

Activity:

1. Open the file **Gallery**.

2. Add your name to the end of the document.

3. Select all of the text using **<Ctrl A>**.

4. On the **Home** tab, **Paragraph** group, click the **Line Spacing** button,

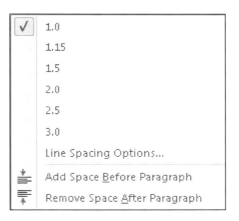

5. Change the **Line Spacing** to **2.0**.

6. Save the document as **spaced**.

7. Change the spacing of the first paragraph to **1.5** lines by placing the cursor anywhere within it and pressing **<Ctrl 5>**.

> **Note:** Press **<Ctrl 1>** for single spacing and **<Ctrl 2>** for double spacing. Use the *numbers on the normal keyboard, not the number pad.*

8. Close the document <u>without</u> saving.

Exercise 35 - Continued

9.   Open the document **Power**.

10.   Select the entire document, and then the **Line Spacing** button.

11.   The last two options refer to paragraph spacing. This document has already had some spacing applied. Select **Remove Space After Paragraph**.

12.   With the document still selected, use the **Line Spacing** button to **Add Space Before Paragraph**.

13.   Click the **Page Layout** tab. Paragraph spacing can also be changed in the **Spacing** area of the **Paragraph** group.

14.   To increase the spacing before the sub title paragraphs only, place the cursor in the text **Solar Panels** and increase the **Before** option to **24pt** by clicking the up spinner.

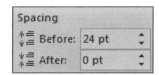

15.   Repeat for the other sub titles.

16.   To leave spacing after a paragraph, place the cursor in the title **Solar Energy** and increase the **After** option to **24pt**.

Note: *To increase the spacing before a paragraph to single line spacing, i.e. 12pt, select the paragraph and press <**Ctrl 0**> (zero). The same key press will remove this spacing before a paragraph.*

---

17.   Close the document <u>without</u> saving.

Exercise 36 - Alignment

Knowledge:

Alignment refers to where text appears on each line in relation to the margins. There are four types of text alignment: **Left**, **Centred**, **Right** and **Justified** (full). Text is normally left aligned or justified (with straight left and right margins).

Activity:

1.   Open the document **Citrus**.

2.   Make the title **Basic Care of Citrus Trees** bold.

3.   Locate the **Alignment** buttons in the **Paragraph** group on the **Home** tab.

4.   With the title still selected, click the **Center** button, ▤, to centre the title.

5.   Select the first paragraph. Click the **Justify** button, ▤. Notice how the text now has straight right and left edges.

> **Note:**   *When text is justified the spacing between words will change slightly. This is quite normal and does not need correction.*

6.   Position the cursor within the second paragraph. Click the **Align Right** button, ▤. As you can see, the paragraph does not need to be selected first, just place the cursor in the text and choose an alignment.

7.   Select the **Align Left** button to see the effect.

8.   Fully justify the remaining paragraphs.

> **Note:**   *To apply alignment using key presses, use <Ctrl L> for **Align Text Left**, <Ctrl E> for **Centre**, <Ctrl R> for **Align Text Right** and <Ctrl J> for **Justified Text**.*

9.   Close the document <u>without</u> saving any changes

Exercise 37 - Indentation

Knowledge:

An indented paragraph is one where the text is further from the margin than the other paragraphs. The <**Tab**> key is used to indent just the first line of a paragraph (hanging paragraph), but the **Increase Indent** button, ▦, on the toolbar is used to indent a whole paragraph. Each time the button is pressed, the paragraph is indented to the next tab stop.

Activity:

1. Open the document **Power** and embolden all headings.

2. Click at the start of the first paragraph, before **Renewable energy**.

3. Press the <**Tab**> key. The first line indents to the first default tab stop position.

Default Tab Stop   *First Line Indent position*

4. Click anywhere in the **Solar Panels** paragraph (not the heading) and indent the whole paragraph to the first default tab stop by clicking the **Increase Indent** button, ▦.

> **Note:** *Press the **Indent** button as many times as necessary to indent the paragraph up to the required tab stop.*

5. Repeat this to indent the **Solar Water Heating** paragraph.

6. With the insertion point still in this paragraph, click the **Decrease Indent** button, ▦, to remove the indentation.

> **Note:** *Increase Indent <**Ctrl M**>. Decrease Indent <**Ctrl Shift M**>.*

7. Indent the fourth paragraph to the second tab stop by placing the cursor within it and pressing the **Increase Indent** button twice.

8. Use the button to indent the fifth paragraph to the third tab stop.

9. Add your name to the end of the document.

10. Close the document <u>without</u> saving any changes.

Exercise 38 - Applying Bullets and Numbering

Knowledge:

Lists and paragraphs can automatically be numbered or bulleted. In each case, a hanging indent is also applied. This means that the first line is further left than the remainder of the paragraph. This separates the text from the numbering and improves the appearance of the document.

If an item is removed from the list, the remaining items are automatically renumbered.

Activity:

1. Open the document **Interviews**. This is a list of job applicants, in the order in which their applications have been received.

    1. Nadine FitzWilliam
    2. Dave Bristow
    3. Malika Ngodo
    4. Terry Colman
    5. Brian Wood
    6. Donna Lavery
    7. Astrid Khan
    8. Paul Vincent
    9. Ian Oliver
    10. Ray Singh
    11. Phil Roche
    12. Jackie Horton
    13. Roger Baker
    14. Kate Hardy
    15. Miles Underwood
    16. Sam James

2. Select all of the text.

3. Number it by clicking on the **Numbering** button, .

4. One of the candidates has withdrawn his application. Delete item number **5**, referring to **Brian Wood**. Notice how the remaining items are renumbered.

5. Close the document without saving.

6. Open the document **Cia Zoo**. Entire paragraphs of text can have bullets or numbers applied.

7. Select all of the text except the title and click, , to apply numbering to each paragraph.

    Welcome to CiA Zoo!

    1. Set in 95 acres of parkland, the Zoo is located four miles north of Learnersville city centre. There are lotsof things to do during a visit. Apart from meeting over 1,200 rare and beautiful animals, you can enjoy many events and activities - ranging from keeper talks to actually being a keeper for a day!
    2. We strive to help ensure the the survival of many threatened animal species and work in partnership with other zoos and conservation projects worldwide. We think it's really important to educate people about wild animals, so they can take an active role in their preservation and conservation. This is why we also work with schools, so that children visiting the zoo todya may become the conservationists of tomorrow.
    3. The zoo is open every day of the year including christmas day and is accessible to visitors with special needs. Please contact us for more information about our facilities if you have special requirements. Parking for 1500 cars is available at the east side of the park|

8. Now select the paragraphs again and click, , to remove the numbering.

9. With the paragraphs still selected, click on the **Bullets** button, , to bullet the paragraphs.

10. Click on the **Bullets** button again to remove them.

11. Close the document without saving the changes.

Exercise 39 - Develop Your Skills

You will find a *Develop Your Skills* exercise at the end of each Skill Set. Work through it to ensure you've understood the previous exercises.

1. Open the document **Chinese New Year**.

2. Change the spacing after each subheading (**Overview**, **The Years**, **Rituals**, **Celebration Food** and **The Home**) to **12pt**.

3. Change the line spacing of the **Overview** text on page 1 to **double**.

4. Indent all text paragraphs to the first tab stop.

5. Save the document as **chinese**.

6. Close the document.

7. Open the document **Muffins**.

8. Change the existing bullets to numbers.

9. Move step 4 so that it becomes step 3.

10. Indent the list of ingredients to the second tab stop.

11. Indent the list of instructions for the **Method** to the first tab stop.

12. Save the document as **muffins3**.

13. Close the document.

Summary: Formatting Paragraphs

In this Skill Set you have aligned paragraphs, added indentation, controlled line and paragraph spacing, and added bullets and numbering.

<u>You should be able to demonstrate your ability to:</u>

- Use paragraph formatting:
    - Line spacing
    - Paragraph spacing
    - Text alignment
    - Paragraph indentation
    - Bullets and numbering

Skill Set 6

Printing

By the end of this Skill Set you should be able to:

Preview Documents

Change Page Orientation

Change Paper Size and Margins

Insert Page Breaks and Paragraph Marks

Create Headers and Footers

Print Documents

Exercise 40 - Previewing Documents

Knowledge:

It is important to make sure a document looks as you expect it to before printing it. **Print Preview** shows the layout of the document.

Activity:

1. Open the document **Citrus**.

2. To preview the document, click the **File** tab and select **Print**.

3. The **Print** screen is displayed. This controls all printing options, but also displays a preview of the document on the right.

4. The print is quite small. Click the **Zoom In** button to enlarge the page.

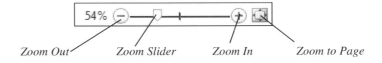

Zoom Out   *Zoom Slider*   *Zoom In*   *Zoom to Page*

5. Click the **Zoom In** button until it shows **80%**.

6. Click the **Zoom to Page** button to return to full page view.

> **Note:** When there is more than one page to the document use the **Next Page** and
>
> **Previous Page** buttons [◄ 1 of 2 ►] to view each page in turn

7. Close the document <u>without</u> saving.

Exercise 41 - Page Orientation

Knowledge:

Page orientation simply refers to which way the document is printed. It can be in

portrait, 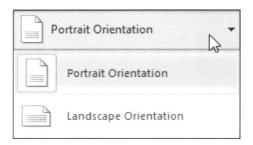, or **landscape**, mode.

Activity:

1. Open the document **Power**.

2. Open the **Print** screen and **Print Preview** the document. It is in **Portrait** mode. This is the default orientation.

3. To change to **Landscape**, in **Settings**, click **Portrait Orientation** to drop down the options.

4. Click **Landscape Orientation**. The preview changes.

5. Use the **Next Page** and **Previous Page** buttons to view all the pages.

6. Click the **Home** tab. Notice that the orientation of the page is reflected on the screen. Depending on your screen size, there may be a horizontal scroll bar allowing movement from side to side.

7. Close the document <u>without</u> saving.

Exercise 42 - Changing Paper Size

Knowledge:

Normally, the paper size you use in *Word* is A4, but because some situations call for the use of non-standard paper sizes, this can be changed. The size selected will depend upon both the printer and the particular application in use.

Activity:

1.   Open the document **Citrus**.

2.   Select the **Page Layout** tab and click **Size**, 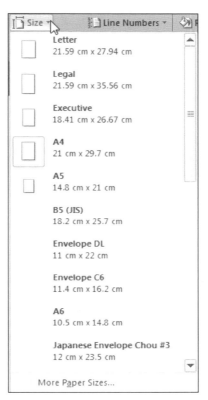, from the **Page Setup** group.

3.   Look at the options available. Some are specialised sizes and refer to American paper sizes (**Letter** for example). Select **A5** from the list.

4.   Preview the document by clicking the **File** tab and selecting **Print**.

5.   On the **Print** screen, locate and click the **Paper Size Setting**.

6.   Change the **Size** to **A4** again. Then, change the **Orientation** to **Landscape**.

7.   Close the document <u>without</u> saving.

Exercise 43 - Margins

Knowledge:

Margins determine the distance between the text and the edges of the paper and are usually the same for the whole document. The top and bottom margins are reserved for features such as headers, footers and page numbering. A large top margin can be set when working with headed notepaper. Side margins can be changed to allow space for binding (**Gutter margin**), to change the length of the document and to improve its appearance.

All margins are, by default, set to **2.54cm**.

Word has a selection of margin options to choose from. They can be changed from the **Page Layout** tab or from within **Print Preview**.

Activity:

1.   Open the document **Property**. This document has **Executive** size applied.

2.   Select the **Page Layout** tab and click **Margins**.

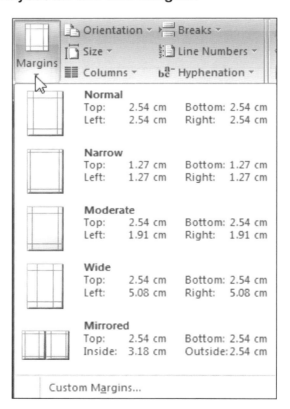

3.   From the displayed list, select **Narrow**. Notice how the text takes up more of the page.

4.   Preview the document. Margins can also be changed from here.

5.   Click the **Margins** button from within **Settings**.

Exercise 43 - Continued

6. Select **Wide**

7. From within **Print Preview** click the **Page Setup** button Page Setup

8. The **Page Setup** dialog box opens at the **Margins** tab.

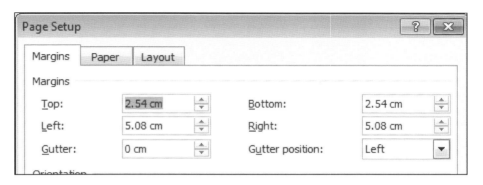

9. The **Top** margin is selected. Type in **2.5**. Press **<Tab>**. The **Bottom** margin is selected. Type in **2.5** again.

10. Change the remainder of the margins to **2.5cm** and click **OK**. The preview changes to reflect the edited margins.

11. Click on the **Page Layout** tab. Open the **Page Setup** dialog box from here using the dialog box launcher in the **Page Setup** group. Click **Cancel** to close.

Note: *If the ruler is not displayed, check the **Ruler** box,* ☑ Ruler *, in the **Show** group on the **View** tab.*

12. Margins can also be changed using the rulers. Adjust the left margin by positioning the cursor over the margin boundary, on the ruler at the top of the screen, until it becomes a double-headed arrow. Drag the pointer to the right. This may take a little while to master – do not choose any of the indent markers.

13. Try holding down **<Alt>** while dragging the margin to the left. The measurements are displayed on the ruler.

14. Adjust the top margin using the boundary at the left of the screen. The pointer will change to a double-headed arrow.

15. Save the document as **property margins** and close it.

Exercise 44 - Headers and Footers

Knowledge:

Headers and **footers** are common identification lines at the top or bottom of each page. They can be displayed on alternate pages, or the same header/footer can be applied to every page. Special automatically updating fields such as the date, time and page numbering can be added to a header or footer.

Activity:

1. Open the file **Buying**.

2. Select the **Insert** tab and from the **Header & Footer** group, select the Header 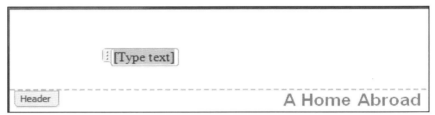 drop down list. From the options, select **Blank**.

3. Notice how the main document becomes ghosted. Click on **[Type text]** (if not selected) and enter **Buying Home Plan**.

4. Click the **Go to Footer** button to switch to the **Footer**.

5. With the cursor at the left of the footer, click **Date and Time** and click **OK** and the current date is added as an automatic field.

6. Press <**Tab**> twice to move to the right of the footer and click **Insert Page Number**. Select **Current Position** and then **Plain Number**.

7. Did you notice that a new tab has appeared while adding Header and Footers: the **Header & Footer Tools** tab with a **Design** option? Click **Close Header and Footer**, from this tab.

8. **Print Preview** the document to check the appearance of the **Headers** and **Footers**.

Note: *Some printers do not print to the bottom of the page, so the footer may not be visible in the **Preview**. To enlarge the **Footer**, display the **Page Setup** dialog box, select the **Layout** tab and increase the setting for the **Footer** in the **From edge** area.*

---

9. Close the document <u>without</u> saving any changes.

Note: *If only page numbers are required then they can be entered from the **Page Number** button from the **Header & Footer** group of the **Insert** tab.*

Exercise 45 - Page and Paragraph Breaks

Knowledge:

In certain situations it may be necessary to start a new page by choice, e.g. at the start of a new chapter, or section of a report. This is known as forcing a new page and is done using a **page break**. A paragraph break is sometimes inserted to split an existing paragraph into multiple ones, or to create a new paragraph when typing.

Activity:

1. Use the document **Buying**.

2. Divide the document into three pages by forcing new pages. Position the cursor in front of the heading **Professional help**, then from the **Page Layout** tab, click ⌷≣ Breaks ▾.

3. Select **Page** from the list.

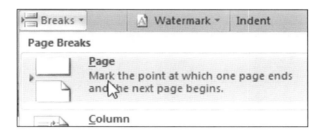

> **Note:** Page breaks can also be inserted by placing the cursor in the correct position and pressing <**Ctrl Enter**> or by displaying the **Insert** tab and selecting **Page Break** from the **Pages** group.

4. Create a second page break in front of the heading **Helping you through the process**.

5. **Print Preview** the document and view the three pages, using **Next Page** or **Previous Page** arrows.

6. Select the **Home** tab to return to the document.

7. On page **2**, a new paragraph is to be created. Place the cursor in front of **Additionally...** in the **Making an offer** paragraph.

8. Press <**Enter**> to create the paragraph.

9. Save the document as **buying3**, then close it.

> **Note:** To remove a Page break it is best to turn on the **Show/Hide** feature, ¶ on the **Home** tab to see the breaks on the page. Then position the cursor on the break and delete it.

Exercise 46 - Printing Documents

Knowledge:

Even though documents can be saved to disk, there may be certain times when you will need to print a "hard copy". There are various printing options available, although you only need to know how to print with the default settings.

Activity:

1. Open the document **Citrus**.

2. Make sure that the printer is switched on, is connected to the computer and loaded with paper.

3. To print a copy of the whole document, click the **File** tab, and display the **Print** page.

4. Click **Print**. A single copy of the document is printed.

5. Close the document <u>without</u> saving.

Print

Note: *The key press* **<Ctrl P>** *opens the print page without using the* **File** *tab. Click* **Print** *to print using the default settings.*

Exercise 47 - Develop Your Skills

You will find a *Develop Your Skills* exercise at the end of each Skill Set. Work through it to ensure you've understood the previous exercises.

1. Open the document **Power**.

2. **Print Preview** the document.

3. From within **Print Preview**, change the orientation to **Landscape**

4. Change the size to **A5** and the margins to **Moderate**.

5. Add a **Header** of **Edited by** *insert your name*.

6. Use the **Page Layout** tab to change the orientation back to **Portrait**, and the size back to **A4**.

7. Print a copy.

8. Place the last paragraph, with its title, on a new page.

9. Make the last sentence a new paragraph.

10. Preview the document again, before closing it <u>without</u> saving.

Summary: Printing

In this Skill Set you have previewed and printed documents, and changed page layout using orientation, margins, paper size and headers and footers. You have also added page and line (paragraph) breaks.

<u>You should be able to demonstrate your ability to:</u>

- Use page layouts:
  - Set paper size
  - Change page orientation
  - Change margins
  - Add headers and footers
  - Add line and page breaks

- Preview a document

- Print a document

Skill Set 7

Creating Tables

By the end of this Skill Set you should be able to:

Create a Table

Enter Text

Inserting and Deleting Rows and Columns

Adjusting Column Width

Delete a Table

Exercise 48 - Tables

Knowledge:

The table feature makes it easy to create documents, such as invoices, that have a tabular format. Tables provide an effective way of presenting tabular data and allow data to be manipulated more easily. Tables consist of horizontal rows, and vertical columns, to create cells like those in spreadsheets. There are some pre formatted tables available.

Activity:

1. Use the key press <**Ctrl N**> to start a new document.

2. Select the **Insert** tab and click **Table**. At the bottom of the drop down list select **Quick Tables**.

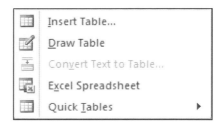

3. From the list of pictures, select **Calendar 2**. Try adding some other tables from the list, to see what is available.

4. Close the document <u>without</u> saving.

5. Start a new document. This will be a created table.

6. The first step is to decide how many cells you need in the table. For this exercise, to create a table with 4 rows and 4 columns, select the **Insert** tab and click **Table**. When the grid appears, move the cursor over the top left cell in the grid, then drag across 4 cells and down 4 cells, as below.

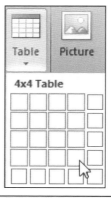

> **Note:** *Alternatively, you can create a table using the **Table** button. Click **Insert Table**, and enter the required number in the **Number of columns** box and the **Number of rows** box (these numbers can be typed in, or the arrows can be clicked to change them). Click **OK**.*

7. Leave the document open for the next exercise.

Exercise 49 - Entering Text

Knowledge:

Once a table has been created, it is simple to enter text and move around within it. It is probably easier to type the text into the table first and then format it, i.e. adjust column widths, etc.

Activity:

1. Use the table created in the previous exercise, the cursor is in the first cell.

> **Note:** Use *<Tab>* to move forward in a table and *<Shift Tab>* to move backwards. The cursor can also be positioned in the required cell by clicking. When entering text, do not use *<Enter>*, unless a new line is required within the same cell, e.g. as in an address.

2. Enter the following text into the table:

Hotel Name	Room Price	Area	Stars
Excelsior	150	Central	5
Grand	110	Central	4
Crusty	50	Outskirts	1

3. Change the room price for Crusty to 45 by editing it in the same way as you would edit in a document. Place the cursor in the correct place, delete 50 and enter the new information.

4. Save the document as **hotel table**.

5. Leave the document open for the next exercise.

Exercise 50 - Inserting & Deleting Rows & Columns

Knowledge:

Occasionally, tables will need to be increased or decreased in size. Rows and columns can be inserted or deleted. Care should be taken when data has already been entered, especially when deleting.

Activity:

1. Use **hotel table**, saved in the last exercise.

2. Place the cursor anywhere in the table. Notice that **Table Tools** are now available with **Design** and **Layout** tabs.

3. You need to add another hotel just above **Crusty**. Click anywhere in the **Crusty** row.

4. Select the **Layout** tab, locate the **Rows & Columns** group and click on **Insert Above**.

5. A new blank row is added. Enter the new text:

    Premium   75   Suburbs   3

6. You decide that the number of rooms should be included in the table. Click anywhere in the **Stars** column. From the **Rows & Columns** group, click on **Insert Right** .

7. A new column is inserted at the extreme right of the table. Enter the title **No. of rooms** and the following in the cells beneath:

    150   127   48   20

8. The **Area** data is no longer required. Click anywhere in the **Area** column. From the **Rows & Columns** group click **Delete**. From the drop down list select **Delete Columns**.

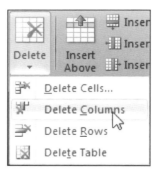

9. You also decide that advertising a poor hotel may not be a good idea. Place the cursor anywhere in the **Crusty** row. Select **Delete** and then **Delete Rows**.

10. Save the document with the same name and leave it open for the next exercise.

Exercise 51 - Adjusting Column Width

Knowledge:

Column width can be altered to better fit the text. Columns can be adjusted one at a time or all together.

Activity:

1. Use **hotel table**, saved in the last exercise.

2. Click inside the table and select the **Layout** tab. Locate the **Cell Size** group. Drop down the **AutoFit** button and select **AutoFit Contents**.

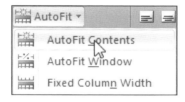

3. The column widths change so that they are just wide enough to fit the widest text in that column.

4. Select **AutoFit** again, but this time select **AutoFit Window**. The table now fits across the page between the margins.

5. Select the whole table by first clicking in it. The **Table Move Handle** appears at the top left corner of the table. Click the crossed arrow to select the whole table.

6. Identify **Table Column Width** in the **Cell Size** group and enter **3.4** to change the widths of all columns.

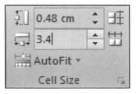

7. Click in the table to make the adjustment.

8. Individual columns can be adjusted using the same method. Click in the **Stars** column and change the width to **1.4cm** using the down spinner.

9. Change each column until you are satisfied with its look.

10. Save the document with the same name and close it.

Exercise 52 - Deleting a Table

Knowledge:

Tables can easily be deleted, if necessary. The method used to delete a table completely is different from that used to delete the content of a table.

Activity:

1. Start a new document and select the **Insert** tab.

2. Click the **Table** button, . Move the cursor across the cells in the drop down panel until a 3 x 3 table is highlighted.

3. Click the mouse button to place the table on the document.

4. Select the whole table using the **Table Move Handle**, .

5. Click the **Layout** tab under **Table Tools**.

6. With the table still highlighted, click the **Delete** button, and select **Delete Table** from the list of options.

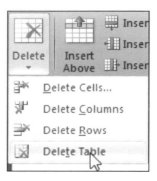

> **Note:** To delete the contents of a table, first select the contents to be deleted, then press **<Delete>**.

7. Close the document <u>without</u> saving.

Exercise 53 - Develop Your Skills

You will find a *Develop Your Skills* exercise at the end of each Skill Set. Work through it to ensure you've understood the previous exercises.

1.   Start a new document.

2.   Create the teacher's timetable below, entering the text as shown.

	Mon	*Tues*	*Wed*	*Thur*	*Fri*
9.00-10.30	7S	11B	8S	8K	9R
10.45-12.15	10F	7L	9R	11B	7L
1.30-2.30	8S	8K	7S	11W	10F
2.45-3.45	11B	7S	10F	11W	11W

3.   Use **AutoFit** to reduce the sizes of the columns to fit the text.

4.   Add a column at the end and title it **After School Activity**.

5.   Change the width of this column to **4cm**.

6.   Use <**Enter**> to add two blank lines after the table.

7.   Insert a **Quick Table** that has a title **Tabular List**.

8.   Use **AutoFit** to make the table fit the width of the page.

9.   Reduce the size of the columns to **4cm**.

10.   Delete the row on **Magazines**.

11.   Save the document as **my tables**.

12.   Close the document.

Summary: Creating Tables

In this Skill Set you have created, modified and deleted tables. You have added and deleted text and numbers, inserted and deleted rows and columns, and adjusted column widths.

<u>You should be able to demonstrate your ability to:</u>

- Work with tables:
    - Create simple tables
    - Enter text and numbers
    - Insert and delete rows and columns
    - Adjust column widths
    - Delete a table

Skill Set 8

Inserting Art and Pictures

By the end of this Skill Set you should be able to:

Insert Clip Art

Insert a Picture File

Use Shapes

Move, Resize and Crop Objects

Exercise 54 - Inserting Clip Art

Knowledge:

Clip Art is a supply of pictures, photos and animations provided with *Microsoft Office*. They are really useful for quickly illustrating your documents and making them more interesting.

To find Clip Art, simply search for a picture in the Clip Art task pane by typing a key word; any matching pictures will be displayed.

Activity:

1. Start a new blank document.

2. Select the **Insert** tab and then click **Clip Art**. The **Clip Art** task pane opens on the right of the screen.

3. Type the word **car** in the **Search for** text box and then click [Go]. After a short delay, a selection of pictures should appear in the task pane.

4. Click on any one of them to insert that image onto the page. Observe the effect.

5. Click on the new image in the document once to make sure it is selected. Then press <**Delete**> to delete the image.

6. Try searching for **rocket**. Insert any Clip Art image that you like into your document.

7. Again, select and delete the new image.

8. Close the Clip Art task pane by clicking the small ⊠ found towards the panel's top right corner.

9. Leave the empty document open for the next exercise.

Exercise 55 - Inserting a Picture from File

Knowledge:

Any picture saved as a file can be imported into *Word*. These images may have been supplied as a collection of photographs on a CD, downloaded from the Internet, or downloaded from a scanner or digital camera. If you are using pictures which are not your property you must be aware of and respect copyright law.

A picture can be placed in a document in two different ways. **In line** means that the picture is placed in a line of text like this, , and behaves like a text character.

Floating means that the picture can be moved anywhere on the page. This is the more useful style because it allows pictures to be placed in any position. The picture on the right is an example of a floating picture.

Activity:

1. Select the **Insert** tab and click **Picture**, Picture.

2. Navigate to the location where the data files for this guide are stored.

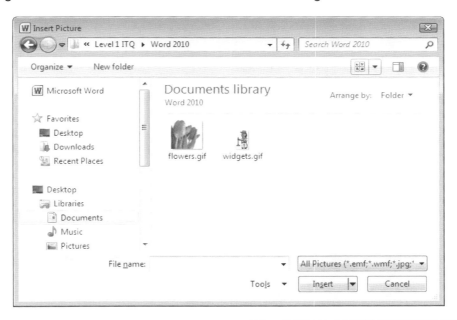

> **Note:** Use the **Change your view** button to change the way the files are displayed. The picture above shows **Medium Icons**.

3. Select the file named **flowers** and click **Insert**. The picture file now appears in the document.

4. Save the document as **art** and leave it open.

Exercise 56 - Working with Pictures

Knowledge:

When an object such as a picture is selected, handles are displayed (small circles in the corners and squares on the sides). By clicking and dragging a handle it is possible to make an object larger or smaller.

Objects can also be moved around by clicking and dragging. First, however, the **text wrap** setting needs to be altered from **in line** to **floating**.

Activity:

1. To resize the flower picture inserted in the previous exercise, first click on it once to make sure it is selected. Notice the squares (handles) around the outline of the picture.

2. Move the mouse cursor over the bottom right handle on the picture so that it changes to a double-headed arrow, 🖎.

3. Click and drag the handle up and to the left, decreasing the size of the picture. Release the mouse button to confirm the change in size.

> **Note:** *Dragging the corner handles of an object changes its size but keeps its relative dimensions the same, i.e. a square will still be square. Dragging the middle handles of an object will deform the shape, i.e. stretch or squash it.*

4. You will have noticed that once a picture is selected, the **Picture Tools - Format** tab becomes available on the **Ribbon**. Click the **Format** tab now.

5. To make it possible to move an object, its text wrapping properties must be changed. Click the **Format** tab and select **Wrap Text** from the **Arrange** group.

6. Select the **Square** wrapping style.

7. Move the mouse over the flowers. The cursor changes to ⊹ when it is in a position to move the picture. Experiment by clicking and dragging the flowers picture to different positions on the page.

> **Note:** *Pictures can be positioned more precisely using the **Position** button.*

8. Click the **Position** button in the **Arrange** group. Then, under **With Text Wrapping**, select the first option (**Position in Top Left**).

9. Notice the effect. Try selecting some of the other options in the **Position** drop-down to see how they change the position of the picture.

> **Note:** *To position a picture precisely, right-click it and select **Size and Position**. The **Position** and **Size** tabs let you specify exact dimensions and alignment values.*

Exercise 57 - Cropping Pictures

Knowledge:

Cropping is used to remove parts of a picture that are not needed. The cropped parts are not deleted and can be restored at any time.

Activity:

1. The flowers picture should still be selected. Select the **Crop** tool from the **Size** group (on the **Format** tab).

2. Notice how the handles around the picture have changed. Place the cursor over the right middle handle. It changes to ⊩.

3. Click and drag the handle left until only the first, pink tulip is visible.

4. Release the mouse button. Then, using the same technique, move the left handle right a little and the bottom handle up a little.

5. Click away from the picture to deselect it. The shaded area is cropped and disappears.

> **Note:** To duplicate a selected picture, use **Copy** and **Paste** from the **Home** tab.

6. Click on the picture again to select it. Then, display the **Format** tab.

7. Drop down the **Reset Picture** button, in the **Adjust** group. Select **Reset Picture and Size** to return the picture to its original size.

8. Save the document with the same name and close it.

Exercise 58 - Using Shapes

Knowledge:

Drawing objects, known as **Shapes**, can be inserted into a document to improve appearance, highlight or add interest when nothing else will do. There are simple shapes, such as rectangles and triangles and more specialized shapes, such as stars, banners and arrows.

Activity:

1. Start a new document.

2. From the **Insert** tab and the **Illustrations** group, select **Shapes**.

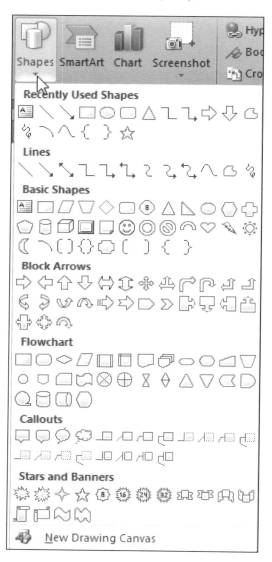

3. Look at the variety of shapes available. Select the **rectangle** from **Basic Shapes**.

4. The cursor now appears on the screen as a cross. Click and drag the rectangle shape on to the page.

Exercise 58 - Continued

5. The **Drawing Tools Format** tab appears, allowing the shape to be changed. There is also an **Insert Shapes** group on this tab. From this group, select an **oval**.

6. Hold down <**Shift**> while clicking and dragging this shape. A perfect circle is formed. This technique can also be used on a rectangle to form a square.

7. Notice how when a shape is selected, or clicked, it has handles, as seen previously. These perform the same function to resize the shape. Also, when the handles are on display the shape can be moved. Click on the rectangle and increase its size by dragging a corner handle outwards.

8. Use a side handle to change the shape of the circle. It now becomes an oval. Click the **Undo** button to reset the circle.

9. Look in the **Shape Styles** group. Click on the rectangle and then the blue square to colour it. Similarly, colour the circle red.

10. Drag the red circle over the blue rectangle until they overlap. All shapes are moved in this way.

11. With the circle still selected click on **Send Backward**  from the **Arrange** group. This is known as changing the order.

12. The circle moves "behind" the rectangle. Click on the rectangle and send it to the back.

13. Hold down <**Shift**> and select the circle. Both shapes are now selected.

14. Click on **Group** and **Group** again from the **Arrange** group.

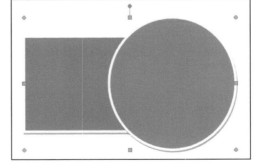

15. The shapes are grouped and can be moved or resized as one.

16. Drag the circle to the left. Both shapes move together. Make the shapes larger using a corner handle of the rectangle. Both shapes are resized.

17. Select **Group** and then **Ungroup** to separate the shapes. Click away from the shapes to deselect them. Reselect the circle and move it away from the rectangle.

18. Try adding more shapes, changing the size, overlapping them, changing the order, grouping and ungrouping them.

19. Close the document <u>without</u> saving.

Exercise 59 - Develop Your Skills

You will find a *Develop Your Skills* exercise at the end of each Skill Set. Work through it to ensure you've understood the previous exercises.

1. Start a new blank document.

2. Change the paper size to **A5** and the orientation to **Landscape**.

3. Use the techniques you have learned to create a promotional flyer similar to the one shown below.

4. The title text is **Brush Script MT 48pt** and is centre aligned and the darkest **Olive Green**. The next line is **Calibri 28pt** and **bold**. The paragraph spacing has been removed from the line **12 The Mall**.

5. The **Clip Art** graphic was found using the keyword search **plumber**. If you are unable to find this graphic, it has been supplied with the data files as **widgets**; insert it from file.

6. Make the **Wrap Text**, of the graphic, **Square** and enlarge it to fit the space.

7. The table is **Calibri 20pt** and is **AutoFit Contents**.

8. Save the document as **plumbers**.

9. Close the document.

Summary: Inserting Art and Pictures

In this Skill Set you have worked with objects and inserted clip art, pictures and basic shapes. You have also seen how to position, resize and crop inserted objects.

You should be able to demonstrate your ability to:

- Insert:
    - Clip art
    - Pictures
    - Basic shapes

- Manipulating art, pictures and shapes including:
    - Positioning
    - Resizing
    - Cropping

Skill Set 9

Checking Your Document

By the end of this Skill Set you should be able to:

Check Spelling and Grammar

Appreciate the Need for Proof Reading

Exercise 60 - Automatic Spell Checking

Knowledge:

Word has a large dictionary (words not in the dictionary can be added). There are two main ways of spell checking. <u>Either</u> spell check while typing, <u>or</u> use the **Spelling Checker** on an existing document.

Misspelled words are shown with a wavy red line beneath them. Green wavy lines refer to grammatical errors.

Activity:

1. Open the document **Cia Zoo**. For now, ignore grammatical errors.

2. If there are red and green wavy lines beneath some of the text, then the **Automatic Spelling & Grammar** feature is already turned on. If it is, **move to Step 6**. If not, perform the following steps.

3. Click the **File** tab and click the **Options** button. Click **Proofing** at the left of the dialog box.

4. Under **When correcting spelling and grammar in Word**, **Check spelling as you type** should have a check mark against it, as should **Mark grammar errors as you type** and **Check grammar with spelling**. If they don't, just click in the appropriate white boxes to insert the ticks.

   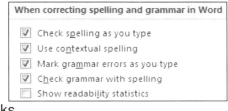

5. Click **OK**. The quickest way of correcting errors is by using the mouse. Place the mouse over the word, **Learnersville** which is underlined in red and click with the <u>right</u> mouse button. A shortcut menu appears.

   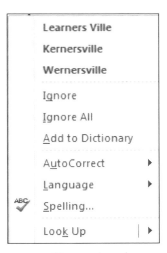

6. Some possible suggestions are given at the top of the list. Clicking one of these suggestions with the left mouse button would add it to the text, replacing the original word, but in this example click **Ignore All** to leave **Learnersville** unchanged (although, as it's a proper name, you could add it to the dictionary, by selecting **Add to Dictionary**).

7. Continue to correct the spelling errors in the same way. There is also a repeated word, **the the**. Select **Delete Repeated Word**.

> **Note:** When text is being entered, a **Spell Book** is shown in the **Status Bar**. If there are mistakes, 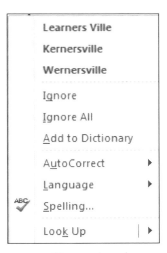 appears, if everything is correct, .

8. Print the document and close it <u>without</u> saving.

Exercise 61 - Spell Checker

Knowledge:

Another way to check spelling is to use the **Spelling and Grammar** dialog box.

Activity:

1. Open the document **Cia Zoo** again.

2. With the cursor at the beginning of the document, select the **Review** tab and click the **Spelling & Grammar** button. The **Spelling and Grammar** dialog box appears.

3. The first (grammatical) error is shown in the top area. Click **Ignore Once** for the green grammatical error for the moment. The next error appears in the **Not in Dictionary** area.

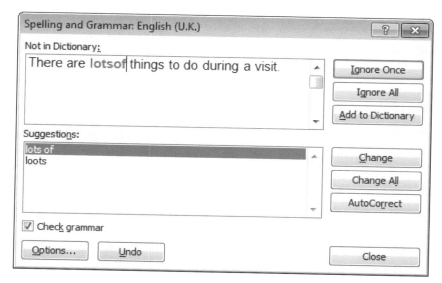

4. Suggested alternatives are shown in the **Suggestions** area. Errors can be ignored, changed or added to the dictionary. Work through the document, making corrections as necessary. For repeated words click **Delete**. The message shown below appears when the check is complete.

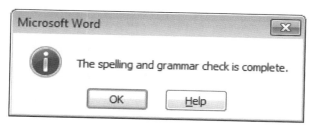

5. Click **OK** and save the document as **cia zoo2** before closing it.

> **Note:** If the word required does not appear in the **Suggestions** box, you can type it into the upper area of the **Spelling and Grammar** dialog box and then select **Change**.

Exercise 62 - Grammar Checker

Knowledge:

Grammar is also checked as text is entered. *Word* makes suggestions which, like spelling suggestions, can be accepted or ignored.

Activity:

1. Open the document **Grammar**. The grammatical errors are underlined in green (it may take a few seconds for the errors to appear after the file is opened).

2. Click the **Spelling and Grammar** button on the **Review** tab.

> **Note:** Notice how the buttons at the right of the dialog box are slightly different to those of spell checking. Make sure the **Check grammar** checkbox is selected at the bottom of the dialog box.

3. The first suggestion amends the word **were** to **was**. Select **Change**.

4. The next suggestion is **I** instead of **Myself**. Select to **Change** this error (perhaps more correctly, this should read **My wife and I**).

5. The next error is an incorrect apostrophe. The correct suggestion is **wife's**.

6. The next error finds an extra space between two words. Click **Change** to accept the suggestion.

7. Click **OK** when the grammar check is complete. Check that the **Spell Book** is showing all complete, ⬛.

8. Save the document as **durham visit** and close it.

Exercise 63 - Proof Reading

Knowledge:

You have seen that *Word* helps you to check your work by means of the spelling and grammar checker. However the spell checker will only highlight words it does not recognise. If you type **horse** when it should have been **house**, the mistake will not be found (horse is a valid word). There is no substitute for a thorough proof reading of your documents. Errors of meaning can slip through the checker and sometimes it makes unsuitable or even incorrect suggestions. When you proof read, you should check spelling, punctuation and grammar, for instance, would a long word be better hyphenated at the end of a line, i.e. split in two? Hyphenation is not on automatically, but must be turned on.

You should also pay attention to the overall presentation and layout of the document. The margins and spacing must be suitable; make sure you haven't used too many different fonts or fussy formatting, as this can make a document difficult to read and can detract from the content. Are the page breaks in a suitable place and do the tables make sense?

Overall you should be looking for consistency and accuracy in your document. That is, is it the type of document required and has the text and other data been entered precisely?

Activity:

1.   Open the document **Proof**. This file has been checked using *Word*'s spelling and grammar checker, but even a glance can tell you that there is still a lot wrong with this document.

2.   Notice the different fonts and colours. Is it easy to read? Read the text carefully. Does the text make sense? What would you do to improve this document?

> **Note:**   *Remember - there is more to checking your work than just spell checking! Check the **Answers** section at the back.*

3.   Would the document benefit from being hyphenated? Select the entire document using <**Ctrl A**>.

4.   From the **Page Layout** tab, drop down **Hyphenation** in the **Page Setup** group. Select **Automatic**.

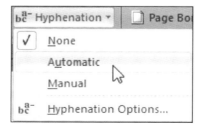

5.   Close the document <u>without</u> saving.

Exercise 64 - Develop Your Skills

You will find a *Develop Your Skills* exercise at the end of each Skill Set. Work through it to ensure you've understood the previous exercises.

1. Open the **durham visit** document.

2. This was spell and grammar checked earlier. Even so, there are still errors in it. Read through and correct any errors you find. They are recorded in the **Answers** section.

3. Save and close the document.

4. Open each document in turn that is in the data folder for this Unit.

5. Spell and grammar check each one before proof reading. Make any appropriate changes.

6. Think about the following:

    Is the text accurate and in the right place?

    Is the text formatted appropriately? – consider font, size and colour

    Are the paragraphs formatted appropriately? – consider alignment, whether numbers, bullets or shading may help, and whether spacing is suitable

    Is the page layout appropriate? – consider the page size, orientation, margins and the page and line breaks

    Are headers and footers in place? – consider the content and placement

    Are any tables, pictures or other objects appropriate and in the right place? – consider resizing or cropping.

7. Preview and then print any that have had exceptional changes.

Summary: Checking Your Document

In this Skill Set you have used the spelling and grammar checker, and learned the importance of proof reading and hyphenation.

<u>You should be able to demonstrate your ability to:</u>

- Check word processed documents by:
    - Spell checking
    - Grammar checking
    - Proof reading

- Understand hyphenation

Answers

Exercise 9

1   Before creating a document, you should think about;

who it is intended for

how it will be used, i.e. hard copy or on screen

is the language suitable

2   a)   Underline
           b)   Show/Hide
           c)   Line Spacing
           d)   Grow Font

3   5 groups

4   Compare

Exercise 63

2   No. The mixture of fonts and colours make the text difficult to read and there are lots of errors (but because they are proper words, for example carp, they have not been marked as errors by *Word*).

To improve the document, you could make the text all one colour and use just one font. The document needs a thorough proof read and corrections need to be made to the spelling and grammar.

Exercise 64

2   Second paragraph should read "awash with boat**s**".

Third paragraph should read "but ~~of~~ **have** to compete with"

Fourth paragraph should read "**Their** boats", and "Their boat**'s** equipment".

Last paragraph, last word should read "**team**".

Glossary

Alignment	Where text appears on the page in relation to the margins.
Application	A software program such as *Word*.
Commands	Selections from the **Ribbon** which perform actions.
Copy & Paste	Duplicate text or objects from one place to another.
Cursor	Indicates where text will be entered when you type (also called the insertion point)
Cut & Paste	Remove text or images, etc. from one place and place them in another.
Font	A type or style of print.
Format	Change the way a document looks.
Headers & Footers	Common lines at the top and/or bottom of each page.
Indent	A measurement by which text is moved away from either the left or right margin.
Margins	The area of white around the edge of the page.
Object	An item imported or created, e.g. picture or drawing.
Orientation	The layout of a page, i.e. **Portrait** or **Landscape**.
Print Preview	Allows a user to see on screen how a document will look when printed.
Save	Keep a copy of your file on the hard or floppy disk.
Template	A base document that contains elements of formatting and alignment and that can be used over again.
Text Wrapping	The formatting that determines how text flows (wraps) around inserted objects such as graphics.
Word Processor	An application for the creation and manipulation of text documents.
Zoom	A feature that either expands or shrinks the view of a document.

Index